Kenwith Castle : and Other Poems

Eliza Down

Copyright © BiblioLife, LLC

This book represents a historical reproduction of a work originally published before 1923 that is part of a unique project which provides opportunities for readers, educators and researchers by bringing hard-to-find original publications back into print at reasonable prices. Because this and other works are culturally important, we have made them available as part of our commitment to protecting, preserving and promoting the world's literature. These books are in the "public domain" and were digitized and made available in cooperation with libraries, archives, and open source initiatives around the world dedicated to this important mission.

We believe that when we undertake the difficult task of re-creating these works as attractive, readable and affordable books, we further the goal of sharing these works with a global audience, and preserving a vanishing wealth of human knowledge.

Many historical books were originally published in small fonts, which can make them very difficult to read. Accordingly, in order to improve the reading experience of these books, we have created "enlarged print" versions of our books. Because of font size variation in the original books, some of these may not technically qualify as "large print" books, as that term is generally defined; however, we believe these versions provide an overall improved reading experience for many.

KENWITH CASTLE,

And other Poems.

BY

ELIZA DOWN.

London:
SAMUEL TINSLEY & CO.
10, SOUTHAMPTON STREET, STRAND.
1878.

LOAN STACK

TO

COLONEL PALMER,

OF TORRINGTON, DEVON,

AS A SLIGHT TRIBUTE OF GRATITUDE AND ESTEEM

These Poems

ARE RESPECTFULLY INSCRIBED.

CONTENTS.

	PAGE
KENWITH	1
BALDER	47
NIGHT AND DAY	52
NIORD AND SKADDA	56
THE NORNS	58
ASGARD	60
THE MESSENGER OF FRIGGA	63
THE GOD OF THE WINDS	64
THE VALKYRS	65
FREY	68
LIFE	72
JAIRUS' DAUGHTER	76
THE MAGI	80
REST	82
THE CROSS	85
"NEITHER DO I CONDEMN THEE"	87
CHRISTMAS, 1877	91
THE NEST	94
MAY..	96
TO A CUCKOO	98
A SUMMER SONG	100
THE BURIED TEMPLE	102
INDIA	108
EVELINE	111

	PAGE
THE BURIAL OF MOSES	114
TO A BUTTERFLY	117
THE THREE KINGS	120
FAILURES	123
THE RIVER	125
THE MOTHER'S PRAYER	127
THE HIGHER AND THE LOWER VOICE	130
ST. PATRICK'S EASTER FIRE	133
JACOB'S DREAM	137
HE GIVETH HIS BELOVED SLEEP	142
MESSERIA	151

KENWITH.

PART I.

WHERE the long channel broadens its blue arm,
Stretched to the main,[1] and rolls its heavy waves
Upon the pebbly girdle of the land,
High on its circular mount, with walls enringed,
Uprose the tower of Kenwith, hoar and grey,
Built by some Briton chief in days far back,
Before the Saxon rose to power of rule;
And therein lay Odune, the Devon Earl,
The servant of King Alfred,[2] and with him
A scanty remnant of his following,
Few men, but brave and of determined soul.
They held the place 'gainst the barbaric hordes
Led by the Viking Hubba, Regnor's son,[3]
Of all the Norsemen fiercest and most fell.

With his long ships, from summer raid returned
From the Demetian coast, which he had swept
With fire and sword, harrying the mountain kings,
He anchored on the Devon shore—a tract
As yet unshorn of its rich growths, where spread
Green pastures, and in season waved, full-eared,
The yellow-bearded corn.   Upon the banks
Washed by the mingled Taw and Torridge ere
They pour their tribute waters to the deep,
The troops of the Berseger camped, and reared
On high their standard ; central 'mong their tents,
The giant ensign waved, its voluminous folds
Opening and closing with the wild sea gales.
Sacred was that great gemmed and broidered flag
To the rude war-sons of the north ; their Scalds
Sang of it in wild lays : fabling, they told
How Hubba, son of Lodbrok, in his youth
Received it, wrought by spell in one brief hour,
By the weird three[4] who in the sombre depths
Of a pine-forest suddenly fronted him
With crownèd brows.   From out the hoary gloom,
Exceeding beautiful of face they shone,

Women, but taller than of mortal mould;
White-raimented, and glistening like the moon,
Silvered with frost. Chanting the runic lay,
They deftly wove—those pale Queens of the North—
The mighty raven standard, gave it him,
And faded out of sight; and evermore
He bore it with his armies where he passed,
Throughout all lands; and ever in the fray
The bird of Odin, wrought thereon by these,
The fateful three, raising the giant wing,
Or drooping it, gave sign of victory
Or loss; in many a field its blazonry
 Had streamed, and round its stand had strove and
   fought
Their noblest, bravest!

      With Odune the Earl,
And with the remnant of his following
Entrenched in the rude fortress, lived that hour
The hope of Alfred's kingdom. The fair land
Lay in the grasp of the rapacious foe,
Sucked dry of all her wealth: northward, from where
Northumbria stretched her line, to the towered city

Built by the Roman lords of old, and thence,
Beyond the streams of Avon, bordering
The land of the West-Saxons, Alfred's seat,
The barbaric troops had poured, and filled
The ways with blood and violence. The Saxon King,
Forsaken of his best in that dark strife,
Stood single 'gainst his enemies, and passed,
Crownless and sceptreless, to the marsh wilds
Of Somerset ;[5] and there, in secret hold
Abiding, tarried till his hour should come
To strike once more for throne and kingdom. Thus
Through all the desolate land one wail went forth :
The glare of temples reddened in the skies,
The peaceful homesteads lay in smouldering heaps,
And still the spoiler spoiled !

       Near ten decades,
The feet of heathen in the land had bruised
Her fields, and trampled down her fruits, at first
Small pirate bands, roving the restless seas,
Which swooped for plunder on the unguarded coast,
Gorged them and fled ; they slowly gathered head,
And waxing bolder, led their armies on

To sack her cities and pull down her forts.
Oft the strong-handed Saxon lords smote them,
But still the hydra-headed foe afresh
Rose up ; and for her slain and vanquished sons,
The teeming North gave from her breast new sons
To more than fill their place !

       Men told of signs
Presaging evil, ere the heathen hordes
Poured from their native forests of the North :
In the night heavens a fiery meteor blazed,
Shaped like a crucifix ;[6] each eve it rose,
After the set of sun, stretching its arms
Athwart the western blue ; upon the disc
Of the blanched moon, paling toward the dawn,
Dark spots like drops of sprinkled blood were seen ;
And on the eve of the Nativity,
The year that Egbert set the regal throne
Above the petty princedoms of the land,
Her broad and silver shield, eclipsed, burned red,
With dusky glare, turned wholly into blood.
And there were wondrous adders in the woods
Of Andreds lea, skirting the Kentish coast,

Where Hengist had his seat of power of old;
Which hissing glid into the homes of men
And wrought them mischief. Thus they spake, and held
Those things prophetic of the direful times
When shrine and altar of the heavenly Christ
Were overthrown and holy place despoiled,
By the red-handed worshippers of Thor.

*   *   *   *   *   *

Within the chamber of the turret sate
The Saxon chieftain, gazing on the sea,
Seen through the lattice of the tower, broad, smooth,
And darkly blue, with all its level waves
Reposed. It was the eve; the sun was low
Upon the waters, and above its disc,
Dark, fiery, hung a single heavy cloud,
Its rough and jagged lines incarnadined
With the red glare beneath. Beside the Earl
A lady stood, of noble mien, his wife;
Her face was white and worn, yet beautiful
As some Greek dream of beauty, like the calm
Grand front of Pallas, with the regal brow
Set with the seal of the high soul. She leant

Upon the chieftain's shoulder, and her eyes,
Like his, were turned toward the great red sun
Slowly descending in the mighty breast
Of waters, crimsoned with the fiery flush
Along the line of waves. Thus for a while
The twain , then, turning to his wife, the Earl
Broke silence, saying, " One sole hope remains—
One only; on it will I stake our all.
Fear not the issue ; we have hewn our way
Through ranks of foes as stout as these which now
Encompass us.

    " Rememberest thou my wife,
That sunrise on the fatal Wilton hills,
The morning after battle ?[7] (Thou wast there,
For all night long thou wanderedst o'er the field
Seeking our Saxon dead.) Not yet the sun
Was risen, but above a pile of clouds
A thin and narrow band of light appeared,
Pale herald of the day. · Then, wearing still
His armour, clotted with the battle-drops,
The King came by, and stood by me and spake:
' What thinkest thou, Odune ; shall in this land

The foe prevail, and all of God be gulfed
In heathen blackness?' and I made reply,
Not wisting what to answer, for mine heart
Was smitten with the sense of our great loss,
'What thinkest thou, my liege?' He answered not
A moment's space; then said he, while his eyes
Rested upon that narrow rim of dawn
Which brightened in the heavens, 'I have thought
' much;

Haply God's purpose broadens slowly through
These bloody times to its full arc of day.
Not Thor, but Christ; not Dane, nor Saxon, Celt,
Nor Angle, but one people in the land,
And in them all the Christ.' Grieving, I spake,
'Oh, my dread lord, how should this be, for we
Are rather like wild beasts that rend each other?'
Still gazing on that line of gold, which waxed
And broadened till the hills were bathed in light,
And all the melancholy field revealed,
With its great clumps of slain, the king replied,
'Methinks it will be so.' He added not,
But as he turned I marked his countenance,

Sublime as some great angel's. Still the words
Live in my mind. Can their fulfilment be?
Or shall this goodly realm of Christ slide back
Upon the edge of hell, and sink itself
Into the bestial slough, knowing not God?
Bruised underneath the Pagan heel we lie.
Oh, England! oh, my country! oh, poor land,
Of thine own sons betrayed!—aliens, not sons.
Shall in the eagle's nest be reared the wren?
Or at the udders of the lioness
Young hares? Yet such are we,—even such."

                                               She bent
Closer toward him, and as he spake her cheek
Waxed paler, whiter than the white storm-foam
Borne on the livid wave. Yet her clear eyes
Shone on him in their beauty, as she said,
"Not all, oh Earl! The winnowing of God
Doth separate the precious from the vile;
Yet are there left some loyal English hearts,
Enough to raise King Alfred's throne once more
From out its ruins,—such thou hast with thee.

These few most noble ones redeem the base."
"Yea," said the Saxon, "there are that remain,
As precious grains in our great heap of chaff;
Nor deem I that the king's high hopes can fail
Wholly their issues. The foul Pagan dark
Cannot out-quench the light. The higher power
Surely subdues the lower. The human doth
Out-tower the brute, and slowly master it,
Though with long steps of pain.

"But to our task.
My men await my bidding; they will go
Whither I lead; yea, into any gulfs
Of death I choose to leap, they will not blench
To follow. We will dare all chance, all risk,
And beard this heathen foe; before the dawn,
Under the covert of the early dusk
Make we our sally from the fort."

He paused,
And all his iron will gathered its power
Upon his massive brows, and set the lines
Sterner round the firm mouth; nor more he spake,
Nor she to him replied. Silent they sate,

Hand clasped in hand, with hearts too passion-fraught
For speech. The mournful sea moaned in her bed,
Rolling from off the beach her tide, and from
The woods a solitary eagle's cry
Resounded in the stillness ;—such great strain
And stress of agony could come but once
Within a life, even as the death-pang
Doth come but once. So the slow moments crept.
And then they spoke, in broken passionate words—
Fragments of speech, shivered with the strong pain,
Like riven stones from the hot entrails thrown
Of fiery Ætna, when its sulphurous womb
Heaves with volcanic birth—their farewells. Rose
They both and stood; then turned, and hand from hand
Lingeringly drew, and the Earl passed from forth
The turret chamber, and the massy door
Clanged after him.

                    Beneath the edge of cloud
The last red embers of the sunset fires
Faded, and the night fell upon the face
Of the broad waters: the pale stars wheeled forth
Upon their courses to fulfil their paths

In the high heavens; the moon was not, or young,
And as a colourless crescent gave faint light
To rip the gloom;—so over all the scene
The descending night her shadowy mantle spread,
Nature's great peace, as ever.

       Then the Earl,
Moving among his followers, spake, "Arise,
Prepare yourselves, for know my purpose stands
To lead you forth. Be ready ere the dawn
Plant her pale prints upon the eastern hills.
Haply we may take by surprise the foe,
Who, haughty in his strength, relaxes watch."

*   *   *   *   *   *

Beneath the raven standard, whose large folds
Swayed slowly in the wind, within his tent,
The Berserk sat, carousing with his jarls.
The bearded vikings grim, lolling at ease,
Filled to the brim the horns with fragrant mead,
Trolling the wassail song from clangorous throats,
While rose and rolled the low hoarse laugh, as breaks
The sullen surf upon the jagged rocks
With all their cavernous hollows!

                    Large of frame
And strong of limb were they, these Norseland jarls :
Upon their arms the brawny muscle swelled,
Like gnarled roots of ancient British oaks,
Knotted and large. Dinted with strokes of war,
Tanned with the winds, those bold sea-rovers; each
Gaunt form was like a furrow-cloven cliff,
On whose keen ledge the eagle sits at watch,
Or like some granite peak far out at sea,
Wave-washed and rent.
                    So drank the Berserk bold
Huge draughts; and all the captains of his war
Drank deep with him, and the wild laugh leapt up,
And rang in peals a-down the table; while
The large and measured horns passed to and fro,
And each man strove his fellow to out drink.
" A goodly land, here will we take our ease:
Large woods and pastures, and fair rivers, where
Glance the bright shoals of fish, tumbles and leaps
The large white salmon, foam-like in the foam !
The Sceptre of the Saxons, where is he ?
Ask the wild boars, question the wallowing swine,

If with them herds the sometime Wessex King."
So passed the scornful jest, tossed like a ball
From each to each, nor spared the Devon Earl,
Late foe in arms, whom with his men they deemed
Meshed in their net. Towered the Norse chief's form,
Uprising; with his heavy fist he smote
Upon the boards, as some huge hammer strikes
Heavily on the anvil of the smith,
And saying, "We have run the fox to earth,
And he cannot escape us," scoffing laughed,
And laid his massive form again at ease.
And when the lazy laughter of his scorn
Died on his lips, lazily he turned him round,
And his eye lighted on his favourite Scald,
Who stood apart, leaning upon his harp.
An aged man was he, with length of beard
In cataracts of snow tossed o'er his breast,
Down to the girdled waist; to him the chief
Spake carelessly, raised on his elbow: "Sing;
Give us one of your sagas; let us hear
The clangour of Thor's hammer as it smites
Upon the rocks, the hurtle and the clash

Of the great gods contending in their halls."
Straightway the hoary Scald bent o'er his harp,
And with his fingers swept the chords, with voice
Accompanying; he sang the ancient strife
Betwixt the Æsir and the giant race,
Waged in the realms of ever-during frost;
And how the hammer of the Thunderer cleft
The mountains to their spurs, rent with their trees
Asunder; and of the great halls of the gods,
And of fair Asgard diademed with towers,
The hundred-gated city which poured forth
Her hosts to battle on the sacred plains,
Her choicest flower of warriors daily slain,
To be with each new morn renewed; then changed,
And like the mournful music of the wind,
'Mong the pine tops, within the vast hoar woods
Of Orkadale, low melancholy flowed
The melodious song, the lay of Balder, first
Of sons of heaven, whom all men did love,
So fair was he, and gentler than the breath
Of spring first breathing o'er her violets.
Howbeit by craft he fell, and the sun-god

Passed to the shades of Hela. All the deep
Burned with the great funereal ship on which
His pallid corse lay decked,⁸ far off it shone,
Like the red meteorous blaze which sometimes lights
The sunless heavens of Norroway in deep
Mid winter—a colossal pyre of fire,
A mount of ruby tipped with gold: while ran
The earth with human tears, more fast than streams
That sudden gush in genial warmth of spring.

But when the strings thrilled to th' impassioned touch,
Suddenly 'neath the hand, the central chord
Snapped, and the music ceased. Then in the pause
Ensuing, lifting up his glooming brows
'Mong the grand rugged heads that ringed him round,
The Scald said gloomily, " An evil sign ;
I like it not, oh jarl ! Sea-king, beware.
The misty remnants of an ominous dream
Trouble my memory ; last night it was,
Methought I stood upon the beach, and gazed
Upon the waters of a turgid sea.
Not this which lips yon belt of pebbly stones

But the great northern sea, with all her waves
Rolled heavily, as after storm scarce sunk
To rest. Above the crest of a large wave,
Hollowed and livid green below, uprose
A head, gigantic, armed, the vizor drawn.
Upon the helm, what seemed a kingly crown
Was set; but as I gazed the circlet paled
And vanished utterly, and the crowned head
Descended crownless to the wave ; strange runes
Ran wailingly along the deep and died
In silence I awoke, and knew my dream
Foreboded evil. Son of Lodobrok
Beware !"

He hearkened, the Norse chief ; his brows,
Like granite rocks o'erhanging scowling floods,
Grew darker in their wrath ; yet light he laughed,
And, striking with his sword on the harp-strings,
Said, " Dream no more—or dream to better aim.
Let the reft chord be mended ; for the rest,
Fear not for us : what the sword wins the sword
Can hold."9

And to his men, " Oh, jarls, rest you,

We verge upon the dawn." He raised the screen
Which parted off the inner tent, passed in,
And on a couch of skins stretched his huge frame;
The fret-work veinage on his temples sank,
And the broad chest to gentler breathings fell,
And gradually as some large braund dies down
From flame to smouldering brightness on the hearth,
The fiery gleams quenched out and paled themselves
In the deep glowing eyes, and with a low
Bubble of laughter, murmuring brokenly,
Half dreaming, "Hares caught in the gin, safe trapped,'
The hardy northern chieftain sank to sleep,
The slumberous thought of scorn within his heart.

PART II.

It neared the dawn, but yet no shafts of light
Pierced the dull east; the swathes of a thick mist
Clung closely to the cold face of the earth;
The leaves were wet as if with heavy rain,
But rain was not, only the sheeted mist
Slowly dissolved itself in clammy drops.

KENWITH.

Within the ancient castle's beetling walls,
The men of Kenwith gathered silently
Around their chief; a single torch,
With foggy rings begirt, burned in the midst,
And cast its light upon the warrior's face,
Revealing it like to some early god's,
Divinely calm: and calm, and stern, and set,
The faces which surrounded him, as if
Hewn from the rock, so stamped was every brow
With steadfast purpose; for they knew, these men,
They moved into the very jaws of death,
Following their leader's call.
       The rivulets
Babbled among their osiers, and the sea
Murmured amid her surges chill and cold.

Then spake Odune, chief of the Saxons, "Rise,
Let us go forth; follow me close, oh friends !
Strike when I give the word. Strike, O great hearts,
For Christ and for the King !" So outward passed,
And underneath the pall of the thick mist
In silent march went on: no clink of sword

Betrayed them, nor the glint of armour shone,
Splintering with rays the dark; no feather waved
In all the band, nor did they bear aloft
The dragon of the western Saxons, which
Their chiefs and heroes old were wont to bear
In battle. As the drops of the night-dew
Softly distil upon the delicate flower,
Soundless their motion; and as silently
And gently as the white curled mist glides up
On a still morn from some smooth river's brink,
Along the grassy marge, they onward moved.
Thus stealthily approached they unperceived
The Norseman's camp. Between the deadly fans
Of the out-lying lines the Saxons passed,
Close to the ring of dusky tents. They crept
On hands and knees along the slimy ground,
Each man apart, slowly, with bated breath,
And with enormous toil. The camp-fires pricked
With spiry flame the dull moist air, and round
About them slept the spearmen of the Dane,
Their arms piled near, while the lax sentinels,
With wassail filled, forbore the wonted watch,

Dreading no foe. So won they way within
The camp of the Dane-King, of him unknown.
The raven standard waved its heavy folds
From the raised staff athwart the shadowy tents,
Dim-gleaming in the dusk, like the white wing
Of some pale swan gliding the azure wave,
The silver broiderings shone on the huge flag
Woven around the bird of the war-gods.
And now from off the bosom of the sea,
With the incoming tide, a breeze began
To rise, which, blowing softly, freshened still,
And the mist lifted as a curtain lifts,
Suddenly, and the dawn smote on the field,—
The chill faint dawn,—revealing the dark orb
Of tents more clear ; and as the obscured morn
Touched with her melancholy rays the plain,
The careless sentinels, sleeping on watch,
Started, and lifting eye, beheld the foe
Close at their side   Then a great cry went forth,
And voices called to arms ; the trumpets brayed,
Hoarse-voiced and deep, and ere the Saxon chief
Could muster round himself his men at arms,

As if the shadowy earth brought forth a crop
Of giant sons, new-sown with dragons' teeth,
The field up-heaved her host of warriors.
Then came he with a shout from forth his tent—
The grim sea-king, the son of Lodobrok!—
A great voice, "Up, jarls, and arm ye! up, Danes,
Kings of the deep!" And shrilled the battle-cry
Of the West Saxons, "Out for holy rood
And for the King!" And Odune formed his men
In order as he best might, being few.
Each Saxon Thane led on his sons and carles.
These, under him, their head formed into close
And narrowed phalanx, forward moved, to make
Assault upon the foe, who, on his part,
Gathered and fronted with great shields enlocked,
Bristling his lines with points of spears. Then charged
The Saxons, and with wedge-like force cleft way
Through the thick hostile ranks. These swerved, and now,
Fierce with great hate, the Dane and Saxon strove,
Man against man, mixed, interwoven, crushed,
In grapple of close fight. So through the morn

The cries of battle rang among the hills
By the grey sea, the while the tardy sun
Arose behind thick bars of heavy clouds,
Between whose openings glared blood-red the light,
As if beneath closed portals slowly oozed
A stream of gore.   And fiercely raged the strife,
Nor ceased, nor slacked, until the Saxon band
Was thinned with slaughter, and the northern jarls
Had, man by man, fallen about their flag.
Then, in the midst of a great ring of slain,
'Mid tumbled helms and shields to pieces hacked,
The Saxon saw his foeman standing.   Proud
He towered his height, unhelmed his head, and loose
His tawny lion-like locks flowed to the wind.
Down at his feet was dropped the large round shield,
Silvered, as the pale moon upon a lake
Uprisen, but his grasp retained the axe,
The dread war-weapon of the northern kings.
Toward him advanced Odune the Earl, nor paused,
Though spent with toils of fight, and dyed with blood
Of heathen, redder than the flame-hued sun,
Which from the shoulders of the enormous clouds

Ascended eastward, while the battle passed
With thunderous shoutings 'long the hilly banks
Skirting the coast.   Over the heaps of dead
The Saxon warrior stepped, and planted foot,
Facing his foe ; nor turned that chieftain grim,
But moveless as a rock awaited him
With front of pride.   But when the Ealdor saw
More near the pallor of the unhelmed brow,
And how the mighty frame, steadfast at first,
Began to sway, as some Norwegian pine
Rocks slowly to and fro, when in a gale
The furious wind tugs at the deep-fanged roots—
(For he was wounded with a grievous hurt—)
The noble heart was touched within his breast
With pity, and, saying, "Oh, mine enemy,
Accept thy life ;" he bent toward him, and threw
Aside with generous hand his orbèd shield.
But the Dane answered not, nor vouched reply,
But knotted into frowns his terrific brows
Heavy with anger.   Suddenly he bowed
Toward the earth, then with swift motion drew
Erect his stature ; on his forehead swelled

The purple veinage, and the muscles rose
Quivering and large on the magnific frame,
Strained to the utmost. Quick he raised the axe,
With fierce two-handed clutch, the knuckles large
And whitened with their grip, hurling his blow
Straight at the Saxon's undefended breast.
But ere the flashing axe, whirling aloft,
Cut through the air descending, Odune saw
The imminent peril, and though waxen faint
With wounds which bled unheeded in the strife,
Stepped quickly back ; but moving, smote his heel
Upon a broken sword-blade on the ground,
And swerved thereby, dropped to his knee on earth,
And over him up-towered the grisly jarl.
In act to strike he stood. when one who served
The Devon Prince came in between the twain,
Shielding his fallen lord from his fierce foe
With the exposure of his own unmailèd breast—
A carle of the Earl's house ; youthful he seemed,
And slender moulded as a woman's was
The supple form in its light coat of hide.
On him, the devoted liegeman, fell the stroke

Aimed at his lord; through nerve and bone it shore
Even to the seat of life. But he who smote
Staggered a step or two backward, and sank
At foot of the great standard of the host.
There lay beneath the shadow of the folds,
And threw his angry eyes upon the Earl
Scowling vehement hate, balked of his prey.
Half from the ground he reared his massive bulk,
Lifted his right arm, and a hoarse sound rolled
Like laughter from his lips,[10] deep volumed, hoarse.
As crashing of the billow when it curls
Its livid greenness in the wild north sea
Into more livid white of angry foam,
So from his lips that laugh. It rolled, and passed
Into the silences of death; he dropped
Heavily forward on the blood-stained ground.

So fell the heathen King before his flag,
And his men panic-stricken fled the field;
As a great mass of snow, hung on the breast
Of some vast Alp, upon a sudden slips
With thunderous sound down to the mountain's base,

The pagans broke and fled; with cries like howls
Of the strong storm in a dense forest where
No foot of man doth come, shrieking 'twixt rows
Of twisted trees: precipitate they fled,
And gat them to their ships moored on the strand,
Nor tarried.
   Over the crushed piteous corse,
A piece of bleeding wreck, of that young slave
Who died to save his lord, bent the great Earl
Grievingly, and with gentle hands unlaced
The tight drawn casque, disclosing the white face
Whose lineaments of most delicate mould
Showed in their native nobleness most pure.
A lovely face was it, crowned with soft rings
Of paly golden curls about the brow—
Lovely yet awful, the smile on the lips
Frozen by death; and the Earl stood at gaze,
Anchoring his steadfast eyes upon its cold
Serenity. He did not stir nor move,
But his face slowly changed, as told in myths
Wondrous of old-world ‘bards, theirs changed who
  looked

Upon the beautiful horror of the face
Gorgonic; cold, stone-like, rigid as death,
Pale as the terrible white polar seas,
When o'er their ribs of icebergs the lean bears,
Shiveringly, in the Arctic winter's cold,
Pass to and fro.   Anon he drew aside
The riven pieces of the leather hide
Covering the mangled flesh, and moving them,
Revealed to sight the breasts of woman, crushed,
Battered, yet visibly the large twin orbs
Female, once lovelier than hills of snow
Or lilies touched with morning's first pale pink.
Upon those mangled breasts the warrior bowed
The grandeur of his head, with a great cry,
Sharp as of one who feels the sword pass through
His loins death-wounded; so he cried and bowed
Lowly the helmèd grandeur of his head.
Anon he raised himself and to his thanes,
Who gathered round in silent reverence,
Noting the greatness of his sorrow, turned,
And saying simply : " It is my wife ; she
Hath followed me into the battle, and given

Her own life for my sake," bowed him again
Over his dead, and his hands wanderingly
Passed o'er the beauty of the face, as one
Blind feels the statue, seeking by the touch
To inform the mind, closed at the gates of sight
From knowledge. O'er the brow and lips and hair
Strayed softly those strong battle-hardened hands,
Dyed with red stains. So long he dumbly knelt
By the crushed body, that the faithful thanes,
Fearing to touch the precincts of a woe
So dread, looked each on each in silent doubt,
Till one approached the Earl, a soldier who
Had loved the Earl his father in old days,
A hard and wrinkled man, but sweet of heart,
And laying on his hand his own, while tears
Dropped from his aged eyes, said: "Dear my lord,
Remember England and the King; to them
As a flower-wreathèd sacrifice to Heaven
Is offered up this sacred woman-life;
Think of it so, and be consoled" The Earl
Lifted himself thereat, and 'neath his feet
The solid earth seemed heaving, as a boat

Rocks underneath the feet of one unused
To the rough dancing of the wild sea's breast;
Yet calmly spake, and curbed th' internal pangs,
As a strong hand controls a wild war-steed
Furious with pain. "Yea," said the Earl, "enough;
Cover from sight the face of my dead wife,
I cannot longer look thereon and be
As man should be. Call back pursuit, and show
Mercy to these the vanquished. To the fort;—
Take up the body, lay it tenderly
Upon your shields, so, let us hence, oh friends,
Sharers of mine heart's sorrow!"

       The grey sea
Rocked in her bed, and lifted up her voice,
Mystic and wonderful.

       So in slow march
Toward the fortress-rock passed on the thanes,
Bearing the noble dead; and 'long the ranks,
From man to man through all the Saxon band,
There went a sound of mourning, like the cry
Of melancholy birds, heard in the night
Flitting across the dim and misty wolds.

And all the women of the castle wept,
Issuing from out the gates [11] to meet the bier
Of their dead lady, and they kissed her face,
Lifting the veil from off the solemn brows:
Kissed it, and wept bitterly, loud and long.'

*   *   *   *   *   *

The night had darkened o'er the battle-field
And o'er the antique tower, and silence was.
Upon the borders of the lonely shore,
The fallen chieftain's grave was made,
And over it was heaped a cairn of stones,
According to the wont of burial
Of the old kings of Northland: in the dim
And clouded night, empty of noises, save
The plashing of the waves upon the beach,
Stood by the grave the Norse chief's ancient scald.
His lean gaunt form was leaner and more gaunt,
All shrivelled as a lightning-blasted pine
Whose bark is bleached and dry; moveless he stood
Within the shadow of the tumulus,
Silently thus a while, and then began,
Moving with measured pace round the grey cairn

To chant a weird, wild rune, mournfully low,
A song, as 'twere, all fraught with human tears.
And when the chant had dragged its length and died,
The ancient saga-man turned from the grave
And bent his heavy steps toward the beach,
Where floated on the waters, large and dark,
The esk of Hubba, with the dragon crest
Carved on the prow, gold scaled, and by its side
The smaller war-craft, empty, silent all,
With idly flapping sails (for they that fled
The sword which hacked them flying, the red field,
Seizing the foremost of their ships, had put
To sea, delaying not). The wrinkled scald
Looked on the large-ribbed barque, and on the line
Of drooping sails shadowing the midnight wave,
With eyes of mournful ire, and murmuring:
"It is the twilight of the gods, the dread
Regnorock, let the great earth rive her sides,
And topple down her cities to the grim shades,
Of mist-swathed Hela," clenched his lean hard palms
Driving the claw-like nails deep in the flesh.

  * * * * * *

Beside the esk a little boat lay moored,
Held by a chain thereto : a slender skiff,
Without or sail or rudder, without oars.
Muttering his words of doom, the saga-man
Approached the boat, and, loosening the chain
Which held it to the esk, he stepped therein.
He stood, he turned, with long lean arms outstretched,
Bending his face toward the burial place
Of the dead King and his fall'n warriors :
" Last of a line of chiefs, from Odin sprung,
Great chief and brave, the Valkyrs call thee up
To feast in wide Valhalla, and to quaff,
From cups of skulls, thine enemies' warm blood,
If that the trumpets of Regnorock yet
Delay to sound the direful day of doom !"
So spake, and pushed the boat from off the shore,
And seaward passed, into the hungry dark,
And no man saw him any more.

       There stood,
Not far removed from the old Castle's seat,
Westering, a hillock ; on its crown a grove
Of trees, which, hearse-like, waved against the line

Of golden cloud, when the great star of day
Rolled on the waters his bright wheels of flame,
Nightly descending. There the wind sang soft
Among the muffling trees, with faint low stops,
A sorrowful hymn, when, as the third morn rose,
Weeping with showers upon the saddened earth,
They laid the lady of Devonia low
Beneath the shadow of the tender boughs,
Wetting the wet earth of her grave with tears.
Pearl of all women, noblest, best of wives,
They named her; not more true Alceste, who,
For love of him she spoused, being great of soul,
Descended to the nether shades, where dwell
The dead of old; nor her made sacrifice
By the rash Gileaditish Prince's vow,
The virgin of Israël, whom Hebrew maids
Yearly with songs lamented. Shine star-like
From the pale night of death, oh noblest name
Of women! The great glory born of thee
Shall light the rim and dusk of aftertime
With radiance, and our sons to be shall call
Thee bless'd. Thus they, the Wessex Thanes,

Their shining armour dimmed with rain of tears;
While women's voices shrilled along the dawn
With funeral music.

                Sorely hurt
With gashes taken in the grisly fight,
Odune the Earl lay stricken nigh to death,
Muttering and wailing ever in his pain,
Unweeting of the things his dry lips spake;
For a great fire burned at the core of life,
And fumed the wholesome brain with mists of dreams
Fantastic. Babbled he of fields and woods,
And pleasant streams that ran by shadowy trees,
The waters lily-snowed; anon, across
The whirling phantasy of his dimmed mind
Terror and darkness drifted the long shriek,
And pass'd the heathen, with a thousand spears
Flashed;—then the dream remade itself to beauty.
So they who listened gathered from his words,
Which told of his own halls, and her who came,
The girl-bride to his home. So tossed and throbbed
The fevered soul. But when the seventh night
Paled its bright moon, wax'd to the perfect shield,

Passing into the grey of earliest dawn,
He raised himself from off the wolf-skin couch,
And leaning heavily on his servant's arm,
Drew to the lattice of the turret-tower,
And gazed therefrom across the dim blue sea, '
Knowing the desolation of his life,
Stripped bare and lone ; weakened, but clear of mind.

He looked upon the wide breast of the sea,
Touched with the first gold of the climbing lights,
And on the bridal earth, veiled in her dews,
While now the fleecy east flushed its red rose
Of dawning (for the rains were overpast,
And in the fields the flowers began to blow,
Faint sweet, and voice of birds was in the groves),
And knew that there had passed from out his life
Its glory, and from the earth and from the seas
Their glory ; yet knew in his deepest soul
That the great purpose of his life changed not,
And wasted not—no, not a single jot.
And as the strong man after sickness runs
His fingers o'er his arm to find if that

KENWITH.

The muscle swell its loops and knots as wont,
Before he close in grapple with his foe,
He felt his higher purpose, and uprose,
God's warrior-servant, ready as erst to strive
In service of the King, against the might
Of heathen breaking flood-like on the land,—
The hordes of Thor.

                Then, ere his hurt was whole,
There went a Bode from the great Earl, and bore
To Alfred, then in hiding in the thick
Of the entangled woods of Somerset,
The tidings of the victory, saying : " Oh King,
Thine enemies are smitten, and their flag
Ravenna taken ; it is in our hands—
The standard of the north, the sign of Thor.
The power of the war-god unto its base
Is shak'n, for the meek Christ doth live and reign
And is the greater !"

                And when the feathery trees
Began to spread the full green fan of leaf
In the far-stretching woods, about the time
Men celebrate the rising from the dead

Of the immortal life,[12] the King went forth,
Leading his followers from their secret hold.
To Egbert's stone he rode; and thither came
To the great forest-heart, the men of Wilts
And Somerset, their thanes and earldormen,
All such as had not fled beyond the seas
For terror of the Pagans; and the King
Cheered them, and heartened them, and, moving through
The dim woods, at the dimly-glimmering dawn
Pitched camp in open space, and there unfurled
His standards, near the wooded heights where lay
The army of the North, under their chief,
Guthrum the aged. Him the Christian King,
Heading his troops, gave straightway battle to,
And drove him back with rout unto his forts.
Then sued for peace the heathen, and their chief,
With thirty of his best, sware to the King
Submission; who received their oaths, and gave
To them large grace and king-like, saying: "Go,
Settle yourselves within our eastern shires;
There dwell in peace, and sow the fields with seed,

And reap their increase ; learn the dignity
Of labour ; live ye there in peace, O Danes,
Serving the Christ under one yoke with us "
So the great Saxon made secure his seat,
Bastioned on truth and righteousness, and built
The greatness of a kingdom up, to rise
Rock-like amid the roll of centuries,
A grandeur of the earth. To him his own
Grew like a fruitful vine ; beneath his sway,
His poor had rest, for those clear eyes discerned
Beneath the peasant's lowly vest, the divine one,
The son of God, though named slave of the soil.
The ever-jarring kinglets of the land,
Who tangled into knots the web of power,
He set at one, and 'neath his guiding hand
Made of their loose divergent sways one whole
Of kingliness, pacific rule and strong,
Perfect as bridal music. His strong arm
Smote the fierce heads of riot, as they rose,
Raised by the lawless heathen from the north
Surging, or lifting up themselves again
Within the realm, and under foot pressed them,

And bruised their power. The sweet arts, flower-like,
Opened, and ampler lights of learning spread
Themselves within the cloisters of the land,
Heretofore darkly wrapped in ignorance.
The East stretched out her hands unto the Prince
Of Saxons, and his pioneers went forth,
Piercing the icy bars of unsunned seas,[18]
Where stream the meteors o'er the shifting bergs,
Varying their splendours. Large his aims and high,
And alway pure; so lived and wrought his work,
And passed, but left behind that work to stand
Thro' all the centuries, a kingdom's base
Of power, until the kingdoms of this world
Pass into the one kingdom of the Christ.

NOTES TO KENWITH.

Note I, p. 1.
"Where the long channel broadens its blue arm,
    Stretched to the main."

The spot which tradition assigns as the site of the old castle of Cynuit (Kenwith), is in the neighbourhood of Westward Ho, on the coast of North Devon, where a long pebbly ridge, extending by the sea-shore, forms one of the most remarkable features of the West of England.

There are no vestiges whatever remaining of the old castle on the circular hill on which it is supposed to have once stood; but this is not surprising, considering the lapse of a thousand years, and the few remains of Saxon buildings of whatever description we possess; for, unlike the Romans who preceded and the Normans who followed, the Celts and Saxons built their forts and castles in the rudest possible manner, and the masonry of the walls of the old fortress of Cynuit, of which Asser writes, wherever situated, would not have been of a character to stand the wear and tear of centuries.

In all likelihood the traditionary site is the correct one, the historical evidence going far to confirm it. It is such a place as some Celtic chieftain or Saxon earldorman might have chosen in the old times whereon to erect his stronghold, from whose turret-tower his glance might sweep the wide breast of the blue waters opening to the broad Atlantic.

Traditions lingering in the locality point to the scene of the battle between the Saxons and the invaders, and to the burial place or tumulus of the Danish chieftain, Hubba, the leader of the Northmen, on the borders of the bay, where the little town of Appledore now stands.

In former years several large stones lay scattered about near the spot, one of immense size, named the Hubba stone, but they have long since disappeared, and only the finger of tradition points to the place where the chief of the wild Norsemen was laid, together with his warriors, by the quiet and wave-washed shore.

NOTE 2, p. 1.

" —— Odune, the Devon Earl,
The servant of King Alfred."

The historical accounts of the Devon Earl are very brief, but sufficient to show him to have been a man of high and fearless soul, a true hero, whom Devonia may well be proud to reckon among the number of those noble sons of whom she has good cause to glory. *Ethelwerd's Chron.* contains a brief mention :

"In the same year (878) arrived the brother of the tyrant Hingwar, with thirty galleys, in the western parts of the Angles, and besieged Odda (Odune), Duke of Devon, in a certain castle."

Asser gives fuller particulars relating to the besiegement of the castle, without, however, mentioning the name of the leader of the Saxons, Odune, the Earldor of Devon. See Asser's *Life of Alfred*, under date of the year 878.

NOTE 3, p. 1.

" Led by the Viking Hubba, Regnor's son."

Hubba was one of the three sanguinary sons of Regnor, a prince of the Danes, surnamed Lodobrok, a personage who figures largely in Scandinavian history and fable, to whom some extraordinary feats are attributed, among others that of slaying a monstrous dragon which encircled with its folds the rock-hewn tower of Thora, a princess descended of the race of Æsir; the hero delivered the captive damsel and took her for his wife. Regnor is said to have met his death in a cruel manner at the hands of Ella, a Saxon chief of Northumbria, and his vindictive sons are supposed to have been actuated with the desire of avenging his death in the cruelties they practised on the Saxon people.

NOTE 4, p. 2.
"The weird three."

I.e. The Norns, or the Northern Fates. They are described as three beautiful maidens who sit by the tree of life and guard it, the great world-tree, whose roots and branches are being continually gnawed, but as continually renewed. They allot the destinies of men.

We find them under another aspect, as the Valkyrs, the three war nymphs of Odin, the choosers of the slain, who are present on the battle-field, and conduct the heroes to the feast in the halls of the gods.

The three weird sisters of Shakspere will no doubt occur to the reader, as well as the three queens of a living poet, each different presentations of the rulers of the secret forces of destiny.

NOTE 5, p. 4.
" —— And passed,
Crownless and sceptreless, to the marsh wilds
Of Somerset——"

At the time when Alfred was forced to seek a hiding-place in the marshy isle of Athelney, in Somerset, the Saxons were reduced to the lowest extremity of misery, the whole country being overrun and pillaged by various bands of the Danes, the dispirited people offering no resistance to the cruel despoilers of their homes. The following from the *Saxon Chron.* will give some faint idea of the state of the unfortunate country.

"878. This year, during mid-winter, after twelfth-night, the army stole away to Chippenham, and overran the land of the West-Saxons, and sat down there, and many of the people they drove beyond the sea, and of the remainder, the greater part they subdued and forced to obey them, except King Alfred; and he, with a small band, with difficulty retreated to the woods and fastnesses of the moors."

NOTE 6, p. 5.

"—— A fiery meteor blazed,
Shaped like a crucifix."

"The sign of Our Lord's Cross appeared in the heavens after sunset," (773) *Ethelwerd's Chron.* See also *Saxon Chronicle*, etc., for this and the other phenomena, which, to the superstitious belief of the Saxon people, were prophetic of the evil calamities of the heathen invasion.

NOTE 7, p. 7.

"That sunrise on the fatal Wilton hills
The morning after battle."

The Saxon arms met a disastrous defeat on the field of Wilton about six years previous to the engagement recorded in the poem.

NOTE 8, p. 16.

"—— All the deep
Burned with the great funereal ship on which
His pallid corse lay decked."

Odin caused the body of Balder the beautiful and beloved to be adorned and laid in state on the deck of a large ship, which was then set fire to. The vessel floated away in flames over the great waters to the regions of perpetual mists. The passing of the sun-browed god to the shades of death is no doubt the symbolization of the going down of the setting sun, sinking amid his fires upon his ocean-bed to the darkness of night.

NOTE 9, p 17.

"What the sword wins, the sword
Can hold."

There is reason to suppose that Hubba contemplated a settlement in Wessex. His brother Halfdene had already portioned out the lands of Northumbria among his followers, and the Danes had effected a settlement in the eastern parts of England, as well as in the midland districts.

NOTE 10, p. 26.
" Lifted his right arm, and a hoarse sound rolled
  Like laughter from his lips."

It was a frequent boast of the wild warriors of the North that they would die laughing Indeed, to them death on the battle-field presented no terrors, but, on the contrary, was a thing to be greatly desired, as it secured an immediate entrance to the halls of Odin, while those who died ingloriously, by reason of sickness or old age, passed to the dolorous vales of Hela.

NOTE 11, p. 31.
" And all the women of the castle wept,
  Issuing from out the gates."

Florence of Worcester states that "Many of king thanes, *with their families*, had shut themselves up in the fortress for protection."

NOTE 12, p. 38.
" And when the feathery trees
  Began to spread the full green fan of leaf
  In the far-stretching woods, about the time
  Men celebrate the rising from the dead
  Of the immortal life.".

I.e. The Easter of 878, a few weeks after the victory of Kenwith, which probably occurred in the month of March

" Meanwhile, after Easter of that year (878), King Alfred fought against the army that was in Chippenham, at a place called Ethandune, and obtained the victory, and after the decision of the battle the barbarians promise peace, ask a truce, give hostages, and bind themselves by oath; their king submits to be baptised, and Alfred the King receives him from the laver in the marshy Isle of Athelney."—*Ethelwerd's Chron.* See also Asser, *Life of Alfred*, Florence of Worcester, and *Saxon Chron.* for fuller particulars of the decisive victory of Alfred over the pagans at this time.

NOTE 13, p. 40.

" The East stretched out her hands unto the Prince
  Of Saxons, and his pioneers went forth,
  Piercing the icy bars of unsunned seas."

Alfred sent help to missions in India, and is said to have sent out explorers to the arctic seas.

BALDER.

Balder the beautiful in Asgard fell;
   Him did all living things swear not to harm,
All trees, all birds, all beasts, were under spell,
   All earth and air owned the great charm!

The mistletoe alone no worship paid
   Of all that breathes, or moves, or greens the earth,
And by its slender shaft was lowly laid
   Of the great heavens the noblest birth!

He fell, and there was weeping in the plain
   Of Ida, and they wept for many days;
He fell, and Hela claimed her prey: not slain
   In war, he passed to her dim ways

And made abode among the dead.   Then spake
  The goddess-mother, she who drew all life
From out her breast, " He will no more awake,
  No more be glorious in the strife

Where gods with giants contend.   Ho! which of you
  Among the doleful shades will seek my son?
Which of you dare dread Hela's gates pass through,
  So that the god from death be won?"

She spoke; then rose Hermode the swift of foot,
  " I will go seek the mighty dead," he said,
" I, even I, will go;" and all the gods stood mute,
  Stricken with grief for him low laid.

He took the horse of Odin, the great steed,
  More fleet than rushing winds; nine days, nine nights,
He travelled through th' abyss, nor slacked his speed,
  Till through the darkness dawned dim lights

Faint, pale, a misty twilight which revealed
  Above a gloomy flood, a single arc
Of mightiest span; the waters lay congealed
  And cold; there never the swift barque

Might pass, or vessel plough the murky wave,
　　The ever-silent river of the dead !
O'er the dread bridge he urged his steed, nor gave
　　One pause till its gigantic head

Upreared, with northern front, the awful gate
　　Of Hela's halls, wide yawned its doors, he passed
Within, then spake the spectral queen, " But late
　　In many a mighty squadron massed

" The countless dead passed o'er yon bridge, yet shook
　　Nor echoed not its arch, but thou did'st make
The crashing thunders roll the deep, thy look
　　Is that of those who joyful wake

" The glories of the strife. Whence comest thou ?
　　And what thy mission here?" He made reply,
" Balder seek I, he of the sun-bright brow,
　　Who wrapped in thy cold mists doth lie !

" Yield back thy prey ; him all the weeping gods
　　Do crave of thee, thou sovereign of the dead !
Behold the nations tremble 'neath their rods,
　　These sue to thee, O queen most dread !"

She answered him, "Weep they? go thou and say,
  Let gods and men, let every creature weep,
Let the whole world run tears, and in that day
  Shall he go free whom else I keep.

"But if one thing refuse to weep, I hold,
  Yea, hold him to the end of days." Then passed
Hermode to the great Odin, and he told
  The words of the pale queen. The vast

And hundred-gated city made one wail
  Of weeping, and the earth wept, and each flower,
Each nestling bird, each beast, all in the dale,
  All on the hills mourned in that hour!

As when the frozen earth, touched by the warm
  Sweet breath of spring makes all her rivers flow,
So ran that rain of tears, yet one wrought harm,
  By malice moved to work them woe

Who dwelt in Ida, weeping not when all
  Gave tears; so the pale Hela kept her prey,
In vain the sacred cities wailed his fall,
  The ages roll,—she holds her sway!

Yet shall he come again and build his throne
  In Asgard, when the days are ripe, there make
His forehead like the sun girt with its zone
  Of rays, and all his prowess take.

NIGHT AND DAY.

"What of the night and day?" he asked
   Who questioned of the sage of old
The secrets of the universe,
   And cause of things, and thus was told:

"Chief of the great primordial powers
   Rose one, a woman giant-born,
They gave her name, Night, dark-browed Night,
   Night of the sable locks unshorn!

"Not then was sea nor land; no star
   Shot forth its ray in heaven; the moon
Hung not its silver lamp on high,
   Nor made the sun its lambent noon.

NIGHT AND DAY.

" 'Mong the frost-giants had she home.
   With one of them she wed ; by him
Conceived, and when her time was come
   Brought forth a daughter, Earth. The dim

" Times spun their course, he died, her spouse,
   Then she espoused one of the race
Of Æsir, and with him 'mong gods
   Made dwelling. Beautiful of face

" Was he ; and unto him she bore,
   Like to himself, a son most fair.
 More goodly child was never born
   In heavenly household ; his bright hair

" Did with a glory crown his brows ;
   He stood before the gods and they
Did own him fair. They gave him name
   According to his nature, Day,

" Sweet Day, the golden bright-browed Day !
   Well pleased the great Al-fader smiled,
And in him took delight ; he smiled,'
   Approval of the beauteous child ;

"And unto him he gave in sign
   Of favour a white wingèd-steed,
And bade him ride in orbits round
   The spacious sky with unslaked speed;

"And to the mother likewise gave
   The kingliest of the Gods a steed,
Coal-black, of mighty moulded limbs,
   Such as might serve untired her need,

"And bear her round the measured space
   In the appointed course. So they,
The mother and the wondrous child,
   Do ever track the selfsame way.

"She first doth ride,—for she was first;—
   And when, her mighty journey done,
She feeds her steed in Ida's vale,
   On the ambrosial food, her son

"Speeds forth; the gleaming gates of Morn
   Open to give him way, he moves
Majestic through the firmament,
   And all his lofty prowess proves,

NIGHT AND DAY.

" In eyes of the beholding Gods.
So run the twain their mighty course,
For thus hath Odin willed, and they
Obey. From the great phantom-horse

" The woman rides, each morning fall
The beaded drops that dew the ground ;
They from the panting courser's bit
Roll down when he doth touch the bound

" And limit of his course. The white
And beauteous steed that Day bestrides
Shakes from his mane o'er heaven and earth
Sweet rays of light, great glory-tides

" Of splendour, brightening all the fields
Of space. So do they keep their way,
Nor swerve aside, nor faint nor flag,
The regent-powers of night and day !"

NIORD AND SKADDA.

Two voices spake,
One of the seas, one of the hills,—
Thus said great Niord the river-God :
"My rest I make
Beside the waters that I love,
Where sing to me the wild white swans.
There do I take
Delight ; how beautiful the seas,
The river's arrowy rush, the spread
Of the smooth lake,
On which the heavens come down with moon
And stars ! in mine own realm I dwell.
Can I forsake
For thee, Oh daughter of the hills,
The wide, free-flowing deep, whose shores

I haunt, to make
Abode with the night-prowling wolves,
With thee among thine own dim hills?"

Then a voice spake;
Thus said the daughter of the hills
In answer: "How can I repose
With thee, and make
My rest upon the sea-god's couch,
When flocks of forest-birds, each morn
Returning, take
Captive my ear with sounds of home?
How can I find delight to dwell
Beside the lake,
Or by the murmuring stream thou lov'st?
No more; get thee a river spouse.
Not for thy sake
Will I forego mine ancient joys.
I bind my skates, I take my bow
Once more, and make
Chase of the beasts that haunt the wilds,
Among mine own loud-echoing hills.

THE NORNS.

By the Udar fount sit
The beautiful Norns,
The mystical nymphs,
With eyes like the morn's.
The tall stately ash
Spreads o'er them its shade,
Yggsbrasil its name;—
From of old they have made
Their rest by the fount,
By the clear-welling spring.
They weave and they shape,
As they eerily sing,
The fates of mankind.

To each nation and race,
To each soul that is born,
They give portion and grace :
And the destinies form
Of the children of time,
With the magical charm
Of their wild runic rhyme.
So dwell the fair three,
By the fountain of life
'Neath the tall stately tree.

ASGARD.

The weird, grand city of the ancient gods.
It towered high up, upon a mighty hill
Of Ida, whose enamelled meads spread wide,
Pressed by the feet of the immortal ones.
Vast were the gates, and huge the girdling walls,
While countless pinnacles pricked the fine air
With spires of throbbing gold, as if the light
Of setting suns kindled them to a blaze;
And over them, upon the topmost ridge
And crown of Asgard, rose a massive pile,
With row of sculptured pillars. The large dome
And stately halls were lightened with the flash
Of glittering swords new-drawn, great brands unsheathed

Perpetually. The large-browed Odin there
Sat on his throne, hearkening the ravens wise,
Which told the secrets of the circled world.
Thor, with his thunders clenched in his strong fist,
And he whose delicate ear, bent at the core
Of Nature's heart, discerned the musical
Soft growing of the grass and fresh green buds,
The rise of wool upon the young lamb's back,
Couched by its dam in daisied meads; with these
In primal golden days passed in and out
The sweet-lipped god, the rosy god of dawn,
Whose fall first cast a shade on Ida's joys.
The warrior-chiefs of earth and Vikings bold,
Who furrowed the rude sea with venturous prow,
Came thither after death, and feasted with
The Æsir, shared with them the listed fight
And tournament. Far off the evil sights
And sounds; not there was heard the howl of wolves
Within the iron wood which lies beyond
Midgard; the scaly dragon's glittering crest,
Coiled in the swathing deep, disturbed not; far
Like thunderous cloud on the horizon's edge—

Far off the glooming of the day of doom,
Regnarock, when the gods with demon-gods
Shall fight, and the huge world roll into dark!
They in Vahalla heed not; wiselier say,
"The tree doth live although the leaf fall off;
Beauty and good do aye renew themselves;
So shall the Æsir fall, yet shall they live.
Evil is but the lower side of good,
So the great wheel shall orb about again!"

THE MESSENGER OF FRIGGA.

The herald goddess through the air
Glided; the Vanir saw and spake:
"'Neath the dim sky what goeth there?
What chariot and courser make
Swift passage through the gloomful night,
With trail like meteor to the sight?"

She said, "With my great steed through air
Thus do I glide, for Frigga spake,
'Go thou;' she is supreme e'en there
Where gods have seats; and I do make
Her will my rule. Thus through the night
I flash like meteor to the sight!"

THE GOD OF THE WINDS.

LIKE to some eagle in a lonely land
Which clasps the rugged peak of the huge crag,
Northward upon the edge of the great heavens
He sits ; he lifts his giant wings, he spreads
His pinions : from them rush earthward the winds.

THE VALKYRS.

The three with helmèd brows shot through the night;
Spectral their steeds, more pale than the wan light
Which lives above the clouded moon. With shield
Uplift they rode, and o'er the direful field,

Where lay the hero-king, fall'n with his dead,
Passed swift. Then spake the chiefest, the most dread
Of the war-nymphs of Odin, first in power
Of these the fateful three which rule the battle hour;

Leaning upon her lance, she spake: "Behold,
The circle of the exulting gods shall fold
One hero more; the prince of men shall bring
His warrior-train to Asgard's halls, and king

"Among the great world-kings shall sit him down."
This heard, where with the glittering jewelled crown
About his brows low lay the smitten chief.
He heard, and to the nymphs thus said in grief:

"Lo! these mine hosts, with them we overthrew,
Have fall'n; one doom hath wrapped us both; we slew,
And slaying, fell. Ye whose pale tresses take
The moony beams as in the wind they shake,

"Ye fates! were we not worthy to achieve
More perfect victory?" Then they: "We weave
The destinies, and we did smite thy foes
With utter loss; we gave strength to the blows

"With which thine arm did quell their pride." Then thus
Gondola to her nymphs: "He gave to us
High charge in synod of the thronèd powers.
Pass we to where vast Asgard rears her towers,

"And say, 'Behold, great Odin, the approaching king;
Him, as thou bad'st us, to thine halls we bring.'
Come, let us urge our steeds o'er the fair worlds
Where roam the mighty gods." They shook their curls

Loose on the wind, and darted through the night.
Then from his halls did Odin send the light,
Swift-footed Hermone, saying: "Go, attend
Upon his way yon warrior-chief, my friend.

"Greet him with honours like a god, and say
The champions in Valhalla wait, and stay
The listed fight that they may welcome thee."
So sent he him, for fleet of foot was he,

And he did pass, swifter than falling star.
Then Hacon came, red with the stains of war;
The starry bosses of his shield were dimmed,
And all his golden armour dashed and grimed

With clots of gore. To him the heavenly powers
Gave welcome large, and where uplifts her towers
The sacred citadel, great Ida's crown,
In circle of the gods he sat him down.

FREY.

Frey, god of fountains and fresh streams, whom men
Invoke for fruitful harvests, he who gives
The soft shower in his season, and the clear
Sweet shining which doth bring the young green blade
To perfect ear, the blossom unto fruit,
Rose from among his fountains and upclomb
The throne of Odin, thence looked o'er the world,
For great is it, a seat built up of old,
Enormous, wonderful. He clomb, and saw from thence
The high-towered cities, river, and spacious plain,
The battle and the goodly pomp of arms;
He saw the great pine-forests, and afar,
The iron coast and murky waves. But where
The mountains of the giants towered and scaled

The northern firmament, the god beheld
A castle seated on a craggy height,
From forth whose portals moved a woman fair
And queenlike, daughter of the giant kings.
Beautiful to sight was she, and from her brows,
Gold-bound, there streamed a light which flamed the lakes
And mountain meres, as when the brazen shield
Of the descending sun its brilliance throws
On the translucent waters. So the god
Beheld her, and his soul went after her
With longing, and he loved. Then was he weighed
With sadness, and he moved through heavenly halls
Silent and mournful, and none wist the cause.

Frey, god of fountains, loved ; no more he found
Delight in hunt or the swift chase, no more
Beside the shadowed streams, as he was wont,
He, flower-crowned, roamed. With passionate desire
His soul was stricken, and he sighed for her—
Gerda, the beauteous maiden of the hills.
He had a weapon famed from ancient times,

A sword which self-directed at his word
Unsheathed itself, and whirling round, bestrewed a field
With carnage. This he took, and spake to one,
A servant of his train: "Go thou and win
Consent of Gerda to become my spouse;
Fairest of women is she, and my soul
Doth languish after her. Go thou and take
For guerdon, if successful, this my sword."
And Skirnir, messenger of Frey, went forth,
And in due time returned and brought his lord
The pledge of Gerda, daughter of the hills,
On the ninth night from thence to wed with him.
In Beri she appointed there to hold
The nuptials, and to keep high festival.
And Skirnir made demand of the great brand,
And Frey did yield it him. Then was he sad,
Th' enamoured god, and went he forth and sate
Among his flowery fountains; and he sighed,
"Long is one night to him who loves and waits
The fruition of his love; more tedious two;
But how shall I endure the third? how wait
Thrice three? The orbing of the crystal moon

Hath often seemed more brief than is to me
This time of waiting!"

                    Thus did Frey forego
His glory as a warrior for love,
Yielding the mighty brand; after he slew
In combat Beli of the giant race,
With branchy antlers of a forest stag;
For he was great of strength, and heeded not
The loss of his good sword. Yet when the days
Of final strife shall come, and conflict with
The anarchic sons of fire, will he repent
He gave away the falchion which did hew
In pieces every foe, self-drawn and aimed.

LIFE.

I walked in woods at Easter-tide,
  And noted how the tender shafts of green
Pushed from the boughs, while far and wide
  Mixed with the delicate moss the wild flowers' sheen
        Spangled the ground!

Waked by sweet touch from sleep, the earth
  Felt her delicious life, and crowned with flowers—
Of her deep heart the glorious birth—
  With throb of joyous wings in all her bowers,
        Sprang to the sound

Of her Creator's voice of love!
  Zoned with her young fresh buds, beauteous and fair,
The mighty mother round her wove
  Still more of life, more rich, more full, more rare,
        The wealth of God!

A while ago, lapped in her snow,
    Like a pale corse she lay, on whose cold lips
The breath plays not, but now the glow
    Of daisies with their tender blushing tips
          Brightened the road!

A while ago, stricken and mute,
    But now her thousand voices carolled forth
Jubilant songs, and like a lute,
    Sweet-toned and tender and of priceless worth,
          Warbling flowed her streams!

Life evermore renewed from death,
    Life in its beauty won from the grim tomb,
With sweetness of the new warm breath,
    Brought forth from out the dark and breathless womb
          ' Of its chaotic dreams.

o real, warm and sweet to touch,
    So beautiful as with the kiss of God!
We shape it still, and dare avouch
    The spiritual thought in us, which looms so broad,
          Substance and power,

The kernel of all outward things ;
　　This vision of the death-won deathless life.
We name it in the Christ, it flings
　　From Him its radiance o'er the awful strife
　　　　　Of our life's hour !

Nor less the thinkers of old time
　　Bodied it forth in legends wild and grand :
The Persian in his creed sublime,
　　The Grecian in the fables of his land,
　　　　　Gave it a being.

Changing and multiform the waves,
　　But one the sea, through all the human tribes
Differing, yet the one truth it saves,
　　And in it all fair hope imbibes,
　　　　　For dimly seeing

The faint day-dawn on the high hills,
　　Watchers in many places as we stand,
We eastward turn, or like the rills,
　　Seaward that flow through all the spacious land,
　　　　　We bend one way.

Hither in Thee the streams are met,
  So think we, Christ, oh living deathless One !
Toward Thee the human still is set,
  Watching and yearning till its goal be won,
    Its summer-day.

JAIRUS' DAUGHTER.

Lay her hands upon her breast :
Oh the rapture of her rest !
Smile the lips as they were wont?—only with a tenderer smile.
Hush ! be still ; surely she but sleeps a little while !

The closed lids of those sweet eyes
Presently will ope and rise,
And their inner lights reveal;— seem they not to quiver now,
As they were about to lift, and those hidden glories show?

But her brow is marble cold,
And her tresses of pale gold

Lie upon her breast, unstirred with its heave or fall.
>> The soft light
Of the silver hanging lamps streams upon that face so white.

>> Woe, alas! for she is dead!
>> Throw the lilies on her bed,
Bid the mourners raise their dirge! weep, oh mother! for your child,
Weep the lately springing hopes so strong and wild

>> Of the coming Kingly One
>> Who the spoils from death hath won,
Healing with a touch the sick, speaking words of mightiest power.
Oh! the hopes, the fears, the passionate longings of that hour

>> When she hung above her child,
>> Though her face was calm and mild
For her gentle darling's sake! Weep, oh! stricken mother, weep;
Shear one tress of hair,—this is all of what WAS THINE to keep.

Hush! weep not, He cometh now!
Mark the sadness on His brow;
And His voice—how full of ruth those low tones of wondrous power,
Sweet to the heart as summer's breath upon the flower!

Can the mournful mother guess
That a love than hers no less,
Greater perhaps, and more divine, lives in Him, the stranger there
That in all that mighty grief He no lesser part doth bear?

By the bed He takes His stand,
The caressing of His hand
Closing o'er the fingers cold, on the lifeless pulseless breast,
The keen watching of His eyes, as He bends, as if addressed

To catch her first faint sigh!
Closer still, and yet more nigh
His face to hers. So the mother o'er her sleeping child
Bends when the morning rays the eastern heavens gild.

My little one, mine own, awake!
Awake, my sweet one, for my sake!
As the babe wakes and laughs back into the mother's face,
So wakes the fair dead maiden at that call of grace!

THE MAGI.

Kiss the dimpled hands ot the infant Christ, oh ye
    aged men !
The first rippling smile of those baby lips is yours ;
    was it then
        For this ye came from far,
        Led by the prophetic star ?

Oh ye sages of the East ! wist ye that a little child,
The high gift of God could be ; discerned ye in that
    infant mild
        Our humanity's true king,
        Who the golden time should bring ?
Turning from the warrior king, with his pageantry of
    power,
To the virgin mother and the babe, in that quiet hour,

THE MAGI.

    Saw ye not the uprising light
    Of the day-spring infinite?

Oh, the woes, the strife of earth, the voice of them that weep!
Hear ye not the bitter wailing voices from the deep?
    Turn and look upon the child,—
    Look into those eyes so mild!

Oh, the shapings grand and dim, in the dreamy Eastern mind,
Of the great restoring one, this is He whom now ye find:
    Yea, behold a little child,
    Look into those eyes so mild!

REST.

THE Christ was sleeping.
On His great amplitude of brow was peace,
    And smiles upleaping
On the calm lips. Hath He awhile found ease,

    The Man of Sorrows?
Hath His great heart fore-gone its bitter toil,
    And bliss, which borrows
All heaven, in dreams, come to Him without soil?

    The waves up-heaving
Break not His rest; the tempest ploughs the deep,
    The wild winds cleaving
Wildly their way over the waters' sweep,

REST.

    But He is resting,—
The Man who wept, who suffered, toiled, and loved ;
    He, who, divesting
Himself of glory, among men still moved,

    Their changeless lover,
Working to ends of changeless love, now rests.
    The storm sweeps over
The vexed and harried deep ; their white foam crests

    The waves are rearing.
Around the sleeping Christ amazed they stand ;
    Such terrors wearing,
The scene appals their hearts. Why doth His hand

    Lie thus all nerveless?
The hand which grasped the seed-germs of the world,
    Which guided, swerveless,
The great life-forces, when all forms unfurled

    To life and beauty.
Peace, ye, and wake Him not. O slow of heart!
    The higher duty
Is faith in that ineffable calm. Your part,

O unbelieving!
Is meek reposing in the unbounded love,
　　From it receiving
Peace in the paths where storm and tempest move.

THE CROSS.

THEY led Him forth without the gates,
When morning dawned upon the city,—
To the high place without the gates,—
    They, the men who knew no pity!

Patient and meek, and king-like still,
All the beauty of His great soul keeping,—
Fainting and weak, yet king-like still,—
    See the strong men round Him weeping!

Bears He to that place the bitter cross,
He, the Christ of our race, the passionate lover,—
Faints He underneath the bitter cross,
    Of all worlds the primal mover!

THE CROSS.

Hangs He there between the earth and heaven,
On the shameful tree in shame uplifted,—
Hangs the dead Christ 'twixt the earth and heaven,
> He, with all great glories gifted!

Lo, the dimmed and bloody sun mourns His death,
Slowly from out its long eclipse passing,
With pale light emerging after His death,
> Where the great clouds are massing.

Behind the darkly looming cross,
The solid rocks are ripped and cleaving,
As if, for sorrow of the cross,
> All Nature's heart was grieving.

"NEITHER DO I CONDEMN THEE."

All in the midnight of her hair
She grovelled at His feet, her fair
White hands crushed under her; she lay
Bruised, helpless, like a flower whose stay
    Has slipped away.

The cruel eyes had turned their scorn
On her, the sinful woman, the forlorn,
Searing e'en to the quivering quick
Of her pained soul, till faint and sick
    She did not reck

Or care if fell the iron shower
To batter her orbed breast that hour!
The torrent roar of a wild woe
Deafened her to the voices low
    Which, speaking slow,

Meted her doom ; she felt, not saw,
The stare upon her shame, so raw
And bleeding; like a trapped wild thing
She quivered, taken in the spring,
    While the close ring

Of bearded men drew closer round
Her cowering form. Then came a sound
As of caged beasts clamouring for food,
More fierce, more savage in their mood
    Than these withstood.

A pause, and then a voice that spake
As though an organ-anthem brake
On solemn silence in the night,
Pealing through aisles all hoar and white,
    Sounds of delight!

"NEITHER DO I CONDEMN THEE."

She felt a hand which lightly passed,
And rested on the tresses massed
On her bowed shoulders; soft it fell,
Soft as the beams which gently tell
  The lily-bell

To waken in the golden morn.
All the fierce clamour of their scorn
Broke fiercer when it fell, that touch,
So soft upon her,—was it much,
  That one avouch

For her the sin-stained woman pity?
They cried, "Cast her without the city;
Hale her unto the stony death;
Batter her till she hath no breath,
  So Moses saith."

Again was heard that voice so sweet,
While she crouched lower at the feet
Of Him that spoke; down on the ground,
Clasping those sacred feet around,
  Making no sound.

Like wind that through a forest goes,
And as its strong tide onward flows
Bends all the trees one way, the power
Of that great voice came in that hour,
    Until the lour

Of evil brows was turned aside.
Silently one by one they glide,
The haughty scribes, from out the place,
Leaving her there before His face,
    Left to His grace.

And over her the tender voice
Said, "Woman sin no more; rejoice
In that the boundless breast of God
Is open, and the heavenly road
    Lies clear and broad."

CHRISTMAS, 1877.

———:o:———

God's greatest, oh Thou little child !
Man's least,—laid with the beasts in stall.
In the high round of heaven the battalions bright
      Sang Thee earth's new-born King !

The shepherds watching o'er their flocks
Saw rising on the dark the sheen
Of Seraph wings, and heard that mighty song
      As torrent waters rolled !

Heard they through the great host the song
Roll on, as trumpet-echoes blown
From cliff to cliff in the deep hollowed heart
      Of mountains in a ring !

Kiss ye the azure-tinted lids
Of the meek babe, rocked to its sleep
Upon the virgin breast; ye shepherds, bend
And worship the young child!

And now we listen, but, alas!
We hear no waft of angel-song,
But shouts of them that strive, the dying groans,
The fallen war-steeds' cries.

The sullen cannon's deadly roar,
And the red leap of angry flame,
The mangled bodies, and the smoking towns,
These are the things that be.

And from across the Eastern seas
The voice of weeping for the dead,
The Indian Rachel mourning for her sons:
Oh! Thou great God, how long!

And yet each day is born anew,
In meekness and in lowliness,
The Christ of God into our world, in shapes
Diverse and multiform.

In deeds of love, of purity,
In all self sacrifice, in all
Great striving after truth, in him who toils,
Or him who quietly thinks.

In him who does a servant's work,
In him who lifts the statesman's voice,
In those who meekly suffer, without word
To speak their suffering.

God's mystery of power is shut
Into low forms, or such we deem
Low forms, yet ever to His clearer eyes
The inner glory shines.

And some there be that hear e'en now
The song of the Great Seraphin
Floating adown the silences of night,—
This night of our earth's woe !

Peal out, and louder, heavenly song,
Burst on our ears this Christmas morn,
On God's high hills ye sing, oh Seraphin !
The Christ new born to men.

THE NEST.

—:o:—

I found a lark's nest yesterday,
I found it in the grass, on the low ground,
   But in the sapphire heights above
The spirit bird, the lark, did make a sound

   Of music, raining down a flood
Of song. On the low ground it had its nest;
   But in the heart of highest heaven
It poured full tide of glorious song: the rest

   So lowly, but the song so high.
Oh bird, oh voice, oh living melody!
   Is it because you build so low
You soar so high? Is thy great ecstacy

Fed from the low earth-source? and hath
The dim sweet mystery of folded life

    In yon small nest filled all thine heart,
Until it overbrims in song so rife

    Of joy, so jubilant, so wild?
I know not; it may be all joy, all love,

    Have lowly source: that earthly love
Feeds that which is divine. To heights above

    All measure love and joy ascend,
Which yet have fountain in most lowly place:

    No poet song but hath its spring
In simplest thing; the sweet home-life doth trace

    Outward its deep divinity
In patriot and sage; no love of child

    But hath its growth toward largest love
Of man. All loves, all feelings soft and mild,

    Do cluster like the sweet rose-leaves
Round the red core, about one central love;

    So mounts the soul on lark-like wings,
So sings, like thee, oh bird! in heaven above.

MAY.

Come with me, love, a-maying !
Come, ere the bees are playing;
Come, while the dew is lying,
And cloud with cloud is vying,
    And lightly floating by,
    In the soft morning sky.
    Come to the flowery mead,
    Where the sweet pleasures lead
The airy dance and mirthful song,
For ever fair and ever young ;
        Come, love, with me !

Sit with me, love, a-maying,
'Neath the white branches swaying,

MAY.

Where the young violet, dying,
Sends out her soul in sighing,
    And breathes of nought but love,
    To the rapt breeze above.
    Here, on a flowery bed,
    Mine heart to thine I'd wed,
And all the sweetness of the May
Pour out in many a tender lay,
        My love, to thee!

TO A CUCKOO.

Oh welcome! welcome to our land,
    Thou spiritual thing!
As silent here I trancèd stand,
    I hear thy voice,
As from a heart of mystery,
    Ringing soft and clear,
Distant, faintly, then more near,
    Floating on the air!
A sweet and artless melody,
    Two notes—no more.

Oh welcome! welcome! and more dear
    Than flowers to spring,
Thou bird unseen! I hear thy voice
    From out the woods,

Or dropping from a cloud on high,
    As thou floatest by,
Through the broad ethereal sky,
    Strangely, sweetly comes
The sound. I hear it and rejoice!

A SUMMER SONG.

Now blows the crimson rose, and the sweet white,
   Now lolls the lily on the silver wave,
Now the full-throated thrush sings to delight
   His brooding mate. The swans their plumage lave,
       Gliding adown
       The azure lake.
Now sweetens in the fruit the tender juice,
   The cherry's ruby clusters ripening glow;
Shakes the laburnum her bright tresses loose,
   While honey-suckles their sweet breathings blow;
       Where shades embrown,
       June's wood flowers wake.

With softest rustlings from the balmy south,
   Young Zephyr comes to fan the dreamy flowers,

A SUMMER SONG.

Sweeter than sweetest kisses on the mouth;
 Led in by meek-eyed Morn, with dewy showers
   Dropped on the meads
   Like orient pearls.
Within the woodland's green and dusky glades,
 The running rivulet laughs and brawls, now leaps
And gleams in sunshine, now glooms in the shades;
 Where the warm sunlight falls subdued and sleeps,
   The fern 'mong weeds
   Lifts its brown curls.

Now in the deep of night, in secret place,
 The nightingale her passionate music pours
On the thrilled air, so hath she only grace
 To sing in silence, and these hearts of ours
   Float into love's
   Own deep divine!
Now, oh dear love of mine, my Psyche sweet,
 With golden zone, gaze in mine eyes with thine,
And let the gorgeous blooms of summer meet
 In our twinned souls, more pure, spiritual fine,
   Than in her groves
   Oh love of mine!

THE BURIED TEMPLE.

---:o.---

    In cavernous gloom,
    Far under the earth,
    A temple doth stand,
    Duskily grand.
Perfect its pillars, and columns, and roof,
Exquisite, delicate traceries gleam on the walls,
Flowerets and fruitage woven in woof,
With the fan of the palm, and the fir trees' dark balls.

    The pomegranates bloom
    As when they had birth
    In the carving's first glory,
    In the dead cycles hoary.

THE BURIED TEMPLE.

Before the high altar the ancient priest waits;
Dark raimented, mournful, and grand,
Keeping watch at the vast sculptured gates,
The old Hebrew prophets silently stand.

>Never light of the sun,
>Or the moon's pale beam,
>Never throb of the star,
>Trembling from far,

Doth shine on that temple so mighty and old.
In cavernous gloom of the deep hollow earth,
It uplifteth its great dome of gold,
There, where never a thing of beauty hath birth!

>Not a motion or tone!
>Like a weird dream,
>The mute white priest,
>The watchers at the east,

The prophets so stern with their grand stony gaze,
Immovable fixed; changeless and still,
Huge shapes in that strange spectral haze,
They loom like the brow of a mist-circled hill!

THE BURIED TEMPLE.

  In the times of the kings
  Who made Israel to sin,
  When the Gentile drew sword
  In the land of the Lord,
When the fierce hosts rolled on like the billows that leap,
To slay and to spoil in the holy place,
The hard earth was cleft to its innermost deep,
And the temple sank, nor left a trace!

  Misty radiance rings
  The dome—a thin
  Pale belt of light—
  Or else would night
Enshroud that mighty temple there.
The gates clang not, nor ever move,
Nor e'er is heard the voice of prayer,
Or music that the Hebrews love!

  No breath, no sound
  Of living thing:
  Ghostly and dim
  In the faint light's rim,

THE BURIED TEMPLE.

The temple of Solomon the wise !
Far down below the summer rills,
For ever hid from mortal eyes,
'Neath the foundations of the hills.

> O'er the charmèd ground
> No bird doth wing
> Its flight, or ever
> Its pinions quiver ;

No foot of man hath ever passed
The dim gigantic porch, or trod
The shadowy outer court, so vast,
Of that wondrous hidden house of God.

> It standeth aye,
> It hath no change ;
> A mystery
> No man may see.

So till the sublime word be given
To bid the buried grandeur rise ;
From the abyss it shall be riven
To tower in sunlight of the skies.

Glorious that day
Through earth's wide range,
From Afric's sands
To the cold northern lands.
The sea shall yield her precious things,
And give her jewels to bestrew the shores,
With low melodious murmurings
She shall pour forth her hidden stores.

On the great mount
Which God shall raise,
And with his hand
Make fair and grand—
With Carmel's grace, and Sinai's weird
Sublimity, with Lebanon's glory,
With cedars crowned—shall be upreared,
Grander than erst, that temple hoary!

Then the Talmudists count,
With its jewels ablaze,
Shall be brought forth,
Priceless in worth—

The crown of the ancient Hebrew kings;
And the Christ shall place it within the shrine:
There, 'neath the spread of the great seraph wings,
The circlet of David shall glitter and shine.

INDIA.

The cry of babes and women—lo, we say,
Four millions hunger: can we part the lump
And take to heart each pining, wailing babe,
Each woman with wan lips, each gaunt worn man?
But God doth so, not we, for unto Him
        Single the sparrow falls,
        The half-fledged raven calls!

Sadder than all the battle-fields these deaths;—
These women with dry breasts, dragged by the mouths
That fain would suck, are more to pain the heart
Than the fall'n warrior gashed with many wounds.
And shall we let them die, we who are set
        The foremost of the earth
        To lead Christ's kingdom forth?

The iron wheels of nature roll and grind
Her faultful peoples ; say they have not learned
Aright her laws, for she hath warned and bid
Them take the larger foresight to provide
Against the evil, but they lived, as lives

   The insect in the bower,
   Fluttering its little hour !

We too are shallow : we have heaped all filth,
All scum within our midst, till the keen sword
Smote for our sin, and with rash hand have let
Our human jewels in our gutters drop,
Our unowned children sink in hells of slush.

   The curse of broken law
   Is ours—stand we in awe !

Oh people ! mighty in the days of old,
Whose sages in the dim gray dawn of time
Fronted with lifted brows the uprising sun,
Ye were a glory in the ancient earth,
And from your lofty natures did evolve

   A creed sublime and grand
   When barbarous was our land.

Yet to be great hereafter, when we wed,
In golden marriage with your antique race,
The vigour of our new, our western strength,
With all that dreamy sweetness which is soul
Of eastern life ; no longer twain that day,

> But one, by the great hand
> Of God conjoined, we stand !

Then shall the kingdom of the future rise,
Like the fine vision of the heavenly mount
Within the prophet's mind—the city of God,
Wherein no evil thing shall come, from whence
Through open gates pour forth the glorious hosts,

> From the great throne, God's river,
> For ever and for ever !

August, 1877.

EVELINE.

My large-browed Eveline !
Tell me, did the great soul,
Which from those eyes of thine
Mingles and melts in mine,
Form with my soul one whole
Of life in some forgotten world ?

For when those eyes divine
Lift on me sudden light,'
Within my mind the fine
And subtle thought doth shine,
As when the fire makes bright
Some dim, weird tracery.   Unfurled

EVELINE.

The past, or mine, or thine,—
Or both,—when some low tone
Trembles, or when you twine,
Like clasplets of the vine,
Your fingers round my own;
Tell me, dear love, what things do make

Such echo-music fine?
What spirit-voices haunt
The hour, oh, Eveline?
The æons that combine
Eternity, and daunt
The mind with vastness, they do take

My large-souled Eveline,
Stand round us, shadowy, dim,
When thou, by flash divine,
Makest my thinkings thine,
Scanning the utmost rim
Of my still thought, to give it life.

Pierce through my soul with thine,
You of the dreamy eyes,

And let the fringes fine,
The skirts of the divine,
Sweep dimly in such guise
Of memory o'er our souls, sweet wife!

THE BURIAL OF MOSES.

SOLEMNLY the shafts of dawning
Lance the shadowy infinite heavens,
Touch the craggy mountain summits,
Pierce the hanging folds of silver,
Strike upon the mournful grandeur
Of the face of the dead prophet!
In the silence and the stillness,
While the pale east slowly brightens,
Flushes into loveliest splendour,
Gold and crimson and vermilion,
Pours the radiance of the dawning
Of the mystic solemn morning,
On the white and sublime forehead
Of the mighty Hebrew ruler.

THE BURIAL OF MOSES.

Swiftly through the vasty spaces,
Through the measureless distances,
Of the golden-clouded heavens,
Shoots a giant dusky figure,
With a smouldering brightness burning
In its folds of vapoury blackness.
With the swooping of the fierce hawk
On the prey in grey of dawning,
Down upon the mountain craglet,
Where the great dead seer reposes,
Swoops the mighty evil angel,
He, the fallen star of morning;
Then from heaven passes downward,
Swifter than the arrowy light-beam
Travels through the endless spaces
Of the mighty countless sun-worlds,
Silent, gently as the snow-flake
On the stainless flower of winter,
The pure Angel of the Highest,
He, the glorious son of morning,
God-like conqueror of evil !

THE BURIAL OF MOSES.

In the silence and the stillness
Of the mystic solemn dawning
O'er the dead form of the prophet,
There upon the lonely craglet,
Spread the great seraphic pinions,
And the evil angel, baffled—
The Abaddon, the Destroyer—
Rolled far off his vapoury blackness,
With the sound of rushing storm-winds,
O'er the seething troubled ocean,
Touching not the sacred body;
For the Angel of the Highest,
He, the guardian of the human,
Who doth watch the seed-germs
Of the deathless and immortal,
Held it safely in his keeping,
Holds it ever in his keeping,
While the ages roll their courses.

Sepulchred by God he lieth
In the deep heart of the mountains,
Guarded by seraphic watchers.

TO A BUTTERFLY.

Come, rest by me,
With gilded wing upon the flower,
And charm me for one fleeting hour!
Come, rest by me,
And make me joyful with the sight
Of an embodied beam of light!

Dear child of spring!
Sweet April's fairest darling thou,
That gently flutterest round her brow,
When from her heart
Goes up through leaf and bud above
The first faint thrill of virgin love!

TO A BUTTERFLY.

Most beauteous thing
That Nature has, how fair thou art,
And yet of strength how small thy part!

One touch of mine
Would brush the beauty from thy wing,
And unto dust thy glory bring!

Great Nature's child,
Go, sport upon the mother's breast!
But for a moment is thy rest.

I own—I feel
A life whose vast immensity
Ages unroll: and yet there be

Some ties which bind
My soul to thee, thou trembling thing.
And there be thoughts untold that bring—

Tremblingly bring—
The tear-drops to mine eyes: sweet thought
And tender memory are brought

Of days long past:
The joy and sorrow of a dream
With thy bright flickering gleam.

TO A BUTTERFLY.

    Creature so frail,
I, that am human, own with thee
Some links of sympathy : to me,
    Sweet wanderer,
Thou art no insect, but a light
From out the past, tender and bright !

THE THREE KINGS.

THERE were three kings with crowns of gold;
They were great and they were bold,
They were mighty kings of old!

With them were courtiers fair and grand,
A glittering and a goodly band,
They rode so gay with hawk on hand!

They stood beneath the greenwood tree,
They laughed and talked right merriliè,
They were a joyful companiè!

Then came a man both old and dree,
Like one from a far countrè;
He bowed him, and thus spake he:

THE THREE KINGS.

"You are three kings with crowns of gold,
You are great and you are bold—
Listen till my tale be told.

"Know ye that I once was fair;
There was naught I would not dare,
When the shield and spear I bare.

"In the joust and in the fight,
I shone in armour silver bright,
I was like a star of light.

"Come ye with me now and see,
Learn ye what the proud shall be,
For you, ah woe! shall fall, like me!"

He spake with words so sad and low,
In such heavy tones of woe,
That they could not choose but go.

To the charnel did he lead,
To the dwellings of the dead,
To the place of woe and dread.

There, in coffins, lay three kings:
All the air around them flings
The stench of putrefying things!

Loathsome, vile to sense were they,
Foul to sight, unfit for day:
Each a rotting mass there lay.

Then spake the man both old and dree,
Like one from a far countrè,
He bowed him, and thus said he:

" Look ye now, oh kings! and see,
Learn ye what yourselves shall be,
For you, ah woe! shall fall like me!"

He ceased: he crumbled into dust
Before their eyes.   Silent and hushed,
They went their way with thoughts more just.

FAILURES.

THERE stood an archer in the dark,
  The arrows of his quiver spent,
Erring, he still had missed the mark,
  Till the last rays of daylight went!

One climbed an Alpine mount when morn
  Reddened the eastward, but the night
Sheeted with mists the glen forlorn,
  Wherein he lay, that youth so bright!

One strove to weave a rope of sand,
  Ghost-like in a dim spectral haze,
For ever to the shadowy land
  Turning the wistful, hungered gaze.

FAILURES.

One crowned with laurel proudly stood,
  Where shoutings rent the thickened air;
Said he, "Is this the promised good,
  This restless throb, this fevered care?"

And one bent grieving o'er the shreds
  Of a waste life—a glorious thing
To tatters rent. When great thought weds
  Great action the sweet angels sing.

Fainting one strove to clasp and win
  The holy vision far away;
Struggling from deepest sloughs of sin,
  Could this, could this be failure, say?

Fainting ere reached the lowest round
  Of the great starry ladder, which
Leads up to God; sought, but not found,
  The Divine, which makes the human rich.

THE RIVER.

—:o:—

Oh, lazy meandering river,
'Tween grassy banks and lolling flowers,
Through all the golden summer hours,
  Flowing on softly ever,
Toward the far-off mighty sea,
What singeth thy low wave to me?

Though lapped in such sweet feeling,
As folds the odorous heart of flowers,
When fed with rains in July hours,
  Some weirdly strange revealing,
Oft dashes the soul's laughter
With shade of the hereafter!

THE RIVER.

Our most delicious dreaming—
Though we do couch on honeyed flowers,
While dance around the rose bright hours—

Is with an innate sorrow teeming,
And from our gleefullest gladness
Start tears with freight of sadness.

Thou flowest on, oh river!
'Tween grassy banks with lolling flowers,
Through all the golden summer hours,

To fall and be for ever
Enwrapped within the infinite sea—
So pass we on to mystery.

THE MOTHER'S PRAYER.

SHE moved from the ranks of the shining ones,
   That mother saintly and white,
She stood at the feet of the Lord of life,
   She stood in the angels' sight,
And unto the heavenly King she said :
   "Oh Father, that lovest all,
I hear the cry of my child in the earth—
   I hear my little one call !
The little one weepeth sore," she said ;
   "He was my joy ; my breast
Did give him suck, my voice at night
   Did lull him into rest ;

But now no hands do fondle him,
　My babe, my tender one!
No eyes do kindle his to smiles,
　My lambkin weak and lone!
Let me go to tend mine hapless babe,
　Till the days when he shall stand
A man 'mong men, noble and strong—
　Let me to yon dim land,
For this return, Father of all!"
　So prayed; and the angel bands
Made pause of song to hear what the Lord
　Should speak, then laid He His hands
On her saintly head, and said: "Not so;
　My daughter abide thou still,
In the realms of light, 'mong my holy ones,
　Tarry thou here secure of ill."
"The little one needeth me," she said;
　"Let me go to tend my child,
For I know that he must suffer woe,
　In life so rough and wild.
The young child weepeth sore," she said;
　"Let me shield my tender one

THE MOTHER'S PRAYER.

From the storm and blast of the bitter earth,
   Till the days of trial be done."
Then the Lord made answer unto her:
   "Oh woman, not so ! behold,
I work my ends through ill to good ;
   Through the damp and heavy mould,
The shafted leaves do push to life,
   From the seed which dies below,
The spiritual flower doth rise and grow,
   With sun-dyed hues aglow !
And through the shapings manifold
   Of suffering and pain,
The human growth attains its end ;
   Nothing is void, nor vain,
For evil doth work the work of good.

THE HIGHER AND THE LOWER VOICE.

Hew down the woods to find the stars !
The axe is slid from out our hands,
  Into the infinite waters.
Sunder the iron prison bars !
The dull corse doth not heed its bonds—
  If men be bound, what matters ?

Soar as the eagle sun-ward soars !
Our life is as the wounded snake,
  Which in the dust doth quiver.
Turn to the east, the golden doors !
Alas ! we wake ; and sleep to wake,
  Haply, no more for ever !

Build we a glory of proud towers?
Our own works dwarf us, and we stand
   Pigmies before their vastness.
Make we a rest within green bowers?
The arrowy rivers through the land
   Run sea-ward in their fastness;

And we, ah whither? Lo, we sit,
Reading a riddle in the dark—
   Born blind, we guess at colours!
And yet our clearer thinkings hit
For evermore one central mark ,
   Amid our dingiest squalors

One perfect image standeth forth—
The divine man, the perfect one,
   The human of the human.
A sublime dream of the whole earth,
Unique in beauty of its own,
   Nor Hebrew, Greek, nor Roman!

Shine out, and clearer, heavenly light,
Rise, sun-like, on the edge of night—

Shine on the waiting nations!
Wax, sun-like, to thy fulness bright,
And to thy clearest noon of light,
　　Lead on the generations!

ST. PATRICK'S EASTER FIRE.

—:o:—

Said the King to his Druids grey,
On the eve of Easter-day,
"See ye the fire on the crown of yon hill,
Red as the sun when the winds are still,
And it riseth in a mist? From the heart
Of the hoary hills the red flames upstart—
What meaneth it, oh! ye wise men say?"

Said the Druids grey to the King:
"Know the meaning of the thing!
The Priest of the pale Nazarene doth light
That great fire in the deep of the night
In contempt of thee, oh King! He doth stand,
Uplifting the cross of the Christ in his hand,
E'en there where the eagle flaps his wing!"

Said the Druids, old and wise :

"See the kindling flames uprise ;
Ruby and golden on high they mount—
He maketh thy word of no account !
Ere the trumpets sound through the silent land,
Ere the word hath passed to the warrior band,

He hath lit his fire—behold with thine eyes."

Said the Druids, like towers of rocks,

That stand the great wave-shocks :
"He hath put to scorn thy kingly throne.
That old man, worn, feeble, and lone,
That single priest of the crucified,
Doth rise against thee in his pride,

And flout thee with his bitter mocks !"

To the Druids grey said the King :

"Look ye into this thing ;
For the man shall die that doth make his fire
Ere our kingly beacon flash, and higher
And star-like rise on the pale night's rim,
From the heart of the mountains vast and dim.

This haughty priest unto us bring !"

ST. PATRICK'S EASTER FIRE.

    Then the Druids went their way,
    That eve of the Easter-day,
To the saintly man on the lone hill crown,
While the glare from the ribs of the rocks upthrown
Reddened the breadth of the eastern heaven,
As when the clouds with the dawn are riven;
    And they told, these weird priests, old and grey,

    The words of their lord the king.
    Like a brooklet murmuring—
A gliding brook when the woods are green—
Flowed the speech from the saintly lips, and the sheen
Of a great light shone on the solemn brow,
As if, with the throb of its glory aglow,
    Quivered above it an angel's wing.

    With the Druids stern he went,
    Stooping with age and bent.
That old man, worn, feeble, and lone,
He fronted the angry chief 'mong his own;
That single priest of the crucified
Spake to the King in his place of pride,
    Of the greater King to this dark world sent!

'Mong the Druids, like towers of rocks
That stand the great wave-shocks—
'Mong the bearded warriors stout and bold,
With shield and lance and chains of gold,
Stood the saintly man, and as to the song
Of a lovely voice they hearkened long,
Nor raised, as he spake, their wonted mocks.

To the Druids grey said the King:
"Wondrous and new is this thing:
The rise of the deathless life from the tomb;
Wondrous the child from the mother's womb—
Each day's new wonder; but this life
More wonderful. Turn we from strife
To Him who life and peace doth bring."

JACOB'S DREAM.

He slept, and over him the Syrian night
  Watched with her stars; around, the mountains
      towered—
On stony pillow slept, far from the light
  Of the loved tent, spread where the trees embowered,
    Beside the smoothly-flowing streams
    Which glassed the morn and sunset beams !

Tier above tier the mighty hills uprose,
  Scaling the infinite skies—peak over peak,
Lifted aloft; all solemn in repose,
  The lonely land : or ere the morning meek,
    Dropping cool dews advanced her way,
    To loose the massy gates of day !

JACOB'S DREAM.

The milky archway shot its lofty span
  Across the sapphire ; the great starry host
Clustered and burned on high—not pale and wan,
  As in our northern climes,—on heaven's high coast
    Fiery or golden, the great stars,
    Arcturus, Orion, Mars,

Shone glorious in the mazy train, and lit
  Th' illimitable vault. On the stilled earth,
With her hushed creatures, a great awe did sit,
  Brooding as 'twere with covering wings : from forth
    That heart of silent mystery
    Issued no sound ; only a tree

Made o'er the sleeper's head a whisper low,
  With waving of its leaves. Wearied he slept,
Forgetful of his toils and all the woe
  Which held his life in travail ; he had wept
    When from his father's house he turned,
    While still his rage within him burned

With smouldering fires half-quenched, for he had bought
  The birthright, as he deemed, but might not take
The purchased prize, nor had he yet one thought
  How mean his craft, while still the wily snake

Of that great sin folded his heart,
With her foul coils o'er every part !

The glory of the heavenly doth arise
   Within the vision of the soul in dreams ;
Shadowed in likeness of the seen ; our eyes
   But look through a thick veil, which hath no seams
     Nor any rent, but whole and one,
     Hangeth before the infinite sun !

We see the type ; but that which lies behind
   The type we faintly guess at. There doth come,
Borne from afar, a whispering like the wind.
   We hear, and name the spirit-voice ; the womb
     Of darkness darkly shuts us in,
     As creatures yet unborn, though thin

The fleshly covering which surrounds our being,
   And hides from us the spiritual. We still
By sense discern the things above our seeing ;
   Upward to God, and his ambrosial hill,
     We climb from the low sensual earth,
     As from dank mould the flower hath birth !

So in the mind of him that slept, the scene
   Of outer glory built itself anew
A spiritual grandeur; as upon a screen
   Reflected, the great heavenly splendours grew
     Within the mirror of that dream,
     Where mystic meanings thickly teem.

From the low earth, where lay the breathing things,
   Where the birds nestled, he beheld a glory,—
A ladder rising with great luminous rings,
   Piercing through the star-spaces white and hoary,—
     A starry ladder great and high,
     Reaching from earth unto the sky!

The lowest round bedded among the flowers,
   But the high topmost shaft hidden in God;
And over it there fell the glory-showers
   Of angels: all along the golden road
     Passed to and fro the angelic throng,—
     The seraphs of the highest song!

And over it and up and down they passed
   Unceasing; he beheld it with his eyes,
This dreamer of old time . along the vast
   Unbroken chain, immeasurable of size,

JACOB'S DREAM.

    Ascending and descending moved,
      God's chosen angels whom he loved!

He saw the astral radiance climb the skies,
  Stretching itself into the infinite,
As mountain peaks one after one arise,
  In a long chain of mounts,—in dazzling light,
    Went up the steps of those great stairs,
    Swept by the breath of heaven's own airs!

From the wet grasses where the young lambs lay
  Went up the glory, up to the high God.
Then saw he how that man might find a way
    Unto the heavenly throne above—
    A ladder knit with links of love!

How man might climb by steps of mountain-stairs
  Unto his Maker, and by starry rounds
Ascend; yea, from the lonely desert lairs
  Scale to the heavenly city's glorious bounds—
    The guarded and the sacred mount
    Whence blessings flow as from a fount!

HE GIVETH HIS BELOVED SLEEP.

She sleeps; we would not wake her—no !
God hushed her to her rest, with low
Whisperings of love. Oh, sleep, not death—
Call it not death !—sweet sleep, life's wreath,
   And crown of balmiest blessing !

For whom the Highest loveth best,
He earliest gathers to His breast.
Like shadowing of an angel's wing,
Soft as the shade, when the young Spring,
   With sweet flowers the earth dressing,

Brings over it an April cloud,
Fell that soft balm of rest. The loud

And turbulent life doth vex our souls :
The mad world's crashing thunder-rolls
  Of battle ; the wild sad moaning

Of an ever-heaving sea of doubt,
Which swathes our isle of life about :
For alway in the mist we stand,
And see not clear His face and hand,
  Who loveth us, still groaning

" He hath forsaken," though He love,
E'en as a mother loves. Sweet dove,
Thou hast found rest within His breast !
Into the calm art passed, and bless'd
  With Christ's own face uplifted,

Rejoicest evermore. Oh flower !
Oh lily of our hearts, thine hour
Was come ! He saw thy bloom, and took
Thee for His lily. Now we look
  On thy bare place. But shifted

Art thou, sweet flower, from earth to heaven ,
For unto thee such grace is given,

To live, dear one, within His sight,
To grow in beauty stainless white,
  Breathing for Him thy sweetness.

Yea, we miss thee much ; our tears
Must flow ; and through the long slow years
Our grief must live, so dear wast thou :
Yet the great peace upon thy brow,
  And thy young soul's full meetness

For Christ and heaven, forbid our grief,
Else wild ; and but a moment brief,
And the thin veil of this our life
Shall part, and we beyond the strife,
  The turmoil and the weeping

Shall pass, and find thee yet again
Our own ; and all the bitter pain
Pass into joy. Meanwhile, rest thou
Beneath the shadowing of God's brow,
  Safe in His holy keeping !

NOTES.

BALDER.

Page 51, lines 1, 2.

" Yet shall he come again and build his throne
    In Asgard, when the days are ripe," etc.

The story of Balder the Beautiful is well known. The goddess Frigga being apprehensive for the fate of her son, took an oath of everything in creation not to do him harm, the mistletoe alone excepted, possibly on account of its insignificance. Loki, the evil one, the contriver of mischief against the gods, having discovered this, causes a shaft made of the mistletoe to be aimed at Balder by one of his companions. The missile effects his death, and as he dies ingloriously, he falls under the dominion of Hela, the goddess of the dead. The mission of Hermode, who is despatched to effect his release, proving a failure through a certain old woman in a cave (who is supposed to be Toki in disguise) refusing to afford the tribute of tears which every other creature gives, he remains under the power of the pale goddess of the shades until the end of time, when it is predicted he will return from the dismal halls of Hela and resume his former glory, restoring the earth, which has been desolated, and establishing universal peace and happiness.

Balder resembles in some respects Apollo, the sun-god of the Greeks, and in others may be compared to Sosiosh, the redeemer of the Persian system. He is the god of eloquence, of music, and of poetry, so fair and beautiful in person that rays of light issue from his forehead, adorning it with a crown of sun-rays. Like the Greek Apollo he endures a long exile from the abodes of the gods.

The myth is one of the finest of the many really fine things of the Northern mythology. In its primary significance it is like most of the myths of the old religions, a shadow from the outward and external on the mind of men. The restoration of the god from the doleful shades of Hela is simply the emergence of the sun in its morning glory from the gloom of night, or the return of spring to the earth after the rigours of winter; and this, grand in its conception as it would appear to the people of the cold Northern clime, has, beyond this, a certain deeper and more spiritual meaning: it speaks of a hope of immortality, of a life utterly imperishable and divine, which must loose the bands of death because it is not possible it should be holden of them.

There is nothing finer in its way than the story of Balder in the whole range of Persian, Hindostanic, or Hellenic myths.

THE NORNS.

Page 58, lines 1, 2.

"By the Udar fount sit
The beautiful Norns."

The three mysterious maidens who have the regulating the affairs of gods and men. They sit by the fountain, under the branches of the sacred ash.

Yggdrasil is of great size, the branches reaching above the heavens, while the roots extend through the whole universe. Both roots and branches are being continually gnawed, the former by serpents, the latter by four harts that are always running across the branches; but the beautiful maidens daily take water from the holy fountain and sprinkle the leaves of the ash, and the tree is preserved in life and verdure. The dews which fall in the vales of earth are the drops which roll from the leaves when sprinkled with the water. The gods daily hold their council under the great ash in the midst of Ida-voll

Yggdrasil is to stand for ever. Even when the world is destroyed, and the Æsir themselves perish, the tree, "Time's hoary nurse," will abide in its pristine bloom.

It is apparently a symbol of universal nature. The whole myth is significant and full of beauty, and is unique in its kind.

ASGARD.

Page 60, lines 11—13.

"The large dome
And stately halls were lightened with the flash
Of glittering swords new-drawn."

In the Edda the hall of Odin is described as lighted up in this manner. The splendid passage in Milton will be recalled to mind .

"Out flew
Millions of flaming swords . . .
. . . . . . the sudden blaze
Far round illumined hell."

It is remarkable the magnificence ascribed to the cities of the Æsir. We read of Odin's halls being roofed with shields of gold, and the palace of Gimli, in which the good are to dwell for ever, is said to be more resplendent than the sun, being adorned within and without with the finest gold. The Scandinavians were not a race of builders, yet they delight in descriptions of the stately palaces of their gods. Probably the great Germanic tribes were wanderers from Asia, who brought with them into Europe some lingering recollections of the grandeur of the ancient cities of the old world, which thus embedded themselves in the traditions of their religion.

NOTES.

Page 61, lines 5, 6

" And he whose delicate ear, bent at the core
   Of Nature's heart, discerned," etc.

I e, the god Heimdall, whose sense of hearing is said to be so acute that he can discern the sound of the growing of the grass and the wool on the back of the sheep. He is the warder of the gods, and is appointed to keep watch at the great bridge Bifrost (the rainbow), across which the Æsir daily ride to the doomstead under the sacred ash. The myth would seem to express that the inner subtle harmony of Nature reveals itself to patient loving observation, that there is a certain rhythm of beauty in the most simple and common of her operations which he who listens can at all times discern.

THE VALKYRS.

Page 65, line 1.

" The three with helmèd brows shot through the night."

The Valkyrs are three warlike maidens appointed by Odin to make choice of those who shall be slain in battle. They are not looked at as evil beings, although endued with attributes of terror.

Hacon, whose virtues and whose triumphant entrance into heaven the Icelandic Scald has seen fit to celebrate, was King of Norway, and flourished in the tenth century.

FREY.

Page 71, lines 9, 10.

" Yet when the days
   Of final strife shall come," etc.

At the end of the world the genii of fire, allied with Loki and the brood of evil monsters, will issue from the fiery region of Muspelhem to make war upon the gods.

The Æsir are overcome, or rather both the evil powers and "the mild gods" mutually destroy each other and bring themselves to an end at the same time; the world is consumed with fire, and the human race perish, with the exception of a solitary pair, who afterwards replenish the earth with their offspring.

The god Balder, after the universal wreck, returns from the abodes of death, and with a remnant of the Æsir will rebuild the sacred cities, and establishing his throne once more restore the earth to more than its former fertility and beauty.

The Eddaic poems give us no idea of an ever-existing and omnipotent deity. The Æsir are rather the life-principles of the universe—the great and beneficent powers of Nature seen in conflict with the destructive and anarchic forces; the Northern sages, however, taught very clearly the immortality of the soul of man.

THE BURIED TEMPLE.

Page 102, lines 1—3.

" In cavernous gloom,
Far under the earth,
A temple doth stand."

There is a tradition in the Talmud that the Temple of Solomon is still existent, concealed in the depths of the earth; and that when the nation of Israel shall be again restored to their own land, it will re-appear as perfect as when first erected on Mount Zion.

At the taking of Jerusalem by Sennacherib, the Rabbis believe the Temple, by the Ministry of Angels, was preserved from destruction by being hidden beneath the earth, where it still remains.

NOTES.

ST. PATRICK'S EASTER FIRE.

Page 133, lines 1, 2.

"Said the King to his Druids grey,
On the eve of Easter-day."

It is related in tradition that St. Patrick converted to Christianity King Leoghire of Ireland, and his nobles, at Easter of the year 433, on which occasion the King held his yearly Court, when he was wont to cause a large fire to be kindled on the top of some eminence, after which his chief men and the people of the country responded with their bonfires in various places. Contrary to the edict of the King, St. Patrick kindled his fire first, thereby proclaiming the Divine King, and perhaps typifying the rising of light from the darkness of the tomb in the resurrection.

LIST OF SUBSCRIBERS.

HER MAJESTY THE QUEEN (2).

THE COUNTESS OF PORTSMOUTH (4).
THE COUNTESS OF CHARLEMONT.
THE LADY GERTRUDE ROLLE (2).
THE LADY CHURCHILL.
THE LADY BRUCE CHICHESTER.
THE RIGHT HON. EARL OF PORTSMOUTH (4).
THE RIGHT HON. EARL OF DEVON (2).
THE RIGHT HON. EARL OF MOUNT EDGCUMBE.
THE RIGHT HON. LORD CLINTON (2).
THE RIGHT HON. LORD COLERIDGE (2).
THE RIGHT HON. SIR STAFFORD NORTHCOTE, BT. (2).
SIR THOMAS ACKLAND, BART. (2).
SIR ARTHUR CHICHESTER, BART.
SIR HENRY DAVIE, BART. (2).
SIR JOHN KENNAWAY, BART. (2).

LIST OF SUBSCRIBERS.

Abbott, Mr., Monkleigh.
Ackland, Dr., Bideford.
Ackland, Mr., ,, (2).
Adams, J., Esq., Bickington.
Adams, Mr., Barnstaple.
Adams, Mr., Crediton.
Adams, Mrs. J., Torrington.
Adams, Mrs. R., ,,
Ainsworth, Mr., ,,
Alford, Mrs. J. Pitton, Barnstaple.
Alford, Mrs. ,, ,,
Allen, Mr., Barnstaple.
Amery, J. S., Esq., Ashburton.
Andrews, Mr. D., Northam.
Andrews, Mr. J., Parkham.
Andrews, Rev. T., Hatherleigh.
Andrews, Mrs., Westleigh.
Andrews, Miss, Torrington.
Arnold, G., Esq., Dolton.
Arthurs, Mr., jun., Rectory, Atherington.
Arthurs, Mrs., ,, ,,
Ascott, Mr., Bideford.
Ashplant, Mr., Torrington.
Ashplant, Mr., Beaford.
Ashplant, Mrs., St. Giles'.
Ashton, Mr., jun., Beaford.
Ashton, Mrs. J., Merton.
Ashton, Mrs. L., ,,
Ashton, Miss M. A., ,,
Atherton, Mrs., ,,
Ayre, Mrs., Southmolton.

LIST OF SUBSCRIBERS.

Babb, Mrs., Barnstaple.
Babbage, Mrs., Bideford.
Babbage, Mrs., Langtree.
Backhouse, T., Esq., Bideford.
Badcock, Mrs., Braunton.
Bailey, Mrs., Buckland Brewer.
Bailey, Mrs., Sheepwash.
Bailey, Mrs., Merton.
Bainton, Rev. J., Bideford.
Bainton, Rev. J., Ilfracombe.
Baker, Mr. G., Appledore.
Baker, Mr., Northam.
Baker, Mr., Barnstaple.
Baker, Mr.,   ,,
Baker, Mr., Bideford.
Baker, Rev. W., Shipton Bellinger.
Bale, Mrs., Bickington.
Ball, Mrs., Frithelstock.
Ball, Miss, Torrington.
Balsdon, Mr , Wear Gifford.
Balsdon, Mrs., Torrington.
Banbrock, Mr., Wear Gifford.
Banbrock, Mrs.,   ,,
Bangham, Mrs., Torrington.
Barnes, Rev. H., Langtree.
Barnett, G., Esq., Ilfracombe.
Barr, Dr., Aldershot.
Barrett, Mr., Torrington.
Barrett, Mrs , Castle Hill.
Barrie, Mr., Stevenstone.
Barron, Miss, Torrington.
Barrow, Miss, Instow.
Bassett, Mrs., Braunton.
Bates, Mrs., Plymouth.

Batson, J., Esq , Ebberleigh.
Baylis, Mr., Pilton, Barnstaple.
Bazeley, H. M., Esq., Bideford.
Bazeley, Rev. F., Bideford.
Beara, Mr , Appledore.
Bedford, Miss, High Bickington.
Beer, Mr , Torrington.
Beer, Miss, ,,
Beman, —, Esq , Croydon.
Bencraft, L., Esq., Barnstaple.
Bencraft, I , Esq , ,,
Bending, Mrs. High Bickington.
Benge, G., Esq., Barnstaple.
Benington, Mrs , Kent.
Bennett, Mrs. Torrington.
Berry, Mr., Pilton, Barnstaple
Berry, Mrs., Ashford.
Besley, Rev. H B. Peters, Marland.
Besley, Mrs., Barnstaple.
Besley, Miss E., Winkleigh.
Best, Mr., Barnstaple.
Bicknell, Mr., jun., Southmolton.
Bidgood, Mr., Instow.
Bilney, A., Esq , Barnstaple.
Bird, Mrs., High Bickington.
Bishop, Mr., Roborough.
Blackmore, Mrs , Kingston-on-Thames.
Blackwell, T., Esq , Barnstaple.
Blake, Mr., Lankey.
Blake, Mrs , Southmolton.
Blatchford, Mr., Hatherleigh.
Blatchford, Mr H., Torrington.
Blythe, Dr., Barnstaple.
Boatfield, Mr , ,,

LIST OF SUBSCRIBERS.

Bolt, Miss, London.
Bolt, Miss, Yarnscombe.
Bond, Mr., Ilfracombe.
Bond, Mrs., Frithelstock.
Bond, Mrs., Monkleigh.
Bonifant, Mrs, Marland
Bonifant, Miss, Torrington.
Boundy, Mrs., Appledore.
Bowden, Mr., Huish.
Bowden, Mr., London.
Bowden, Mrs., Appledore.
Bowen, Mrs, Bideford.
Boxer, Mr., Torrington.
Boyden, Mr., Bristol.
Boyles, Mr., Bideford.
Bradford, Mrs., Torrington.
Brailey, Mr., Ashford.
Brailey, Mrs, Exeter.
Braithwaite, Rev. C. F., Southmolton.
Braund, Mr., Bideford.
Braund, Mr., Hatherleigh.
Braund, Mr., jun., Little Torrington.
Braund, Mr., jun , Ilfracombe.
Braund, Mrs., Fremington.
Bray, Mr., Bideford.
Bray, Mrs., Barnstaple.
Brenton, Rev. J., Southmolton.
Brereton, A., Esq., Liverpool.
Brereton, O., Esq.,   ,,
Brereton, A. J., Esq., Mold.
Bridgeman, Mrs., Shebear.
Brierly, Rev. J., Leytonstone.
Brimsmead, Miss, Newport, Mon.
Brindle, Rev. Provost, Barnstaple.

LIST OF SUBSCRIBERS.

Brinsmead, Mr, London.
Brinsmead, Mr., St Giles'.
Brock, Mr., Bideford.
Bounscombe, Mr. E., Hunshaw.
Brounscombe, Mrs., High Bickington.
Brown, G, Esq, Barnstaple.
Brown, Mr., Barnstaple.
Bryant, Mr., Barnstaple.
Buckingham, Mr, Barnstaple
Buckingham, Mr., Lankey.
Buckinham, W., Esq., Exeter.
Buckland, Rev. S., Torrington.
Buckland, Mis, Croydon
Buckpitt, J., Esq, Taunton.
Budd, Dr, Barnstaple.
Bull, Rev J. H., Barnstaple.
Bullied, Mr., Hatherleigh.
Bullied, Mr. J.,   ,,
Bullied, Mr S,   ,,
Bulmer, Mr., Southmolton.
Buncombe, W., Esq, High Bickington.
Burrington, F., Esq., Exeter.
Burrows, Mrs, Frithelstock.
Burton, Mrs., Exeter.
Buttard, Mrs., Instow.

Caddy, Miss, Buckland Brewer.
Callard, Miss, Yarnscombe.
Campbell, E., Esq, Westward Ho!
Cann, Mr, Alverdiscott.
Cann, Mr., Torrington.
Capern, E., Esq., Birmingham.
Carew, T., Esq, Tiverton.
Carter, Mrs., Torrington.

LIST OF SUBSCRIBERS.

Cato, Mr., Merton.
Cawker, Mrs., Swansea (2).
Chamings, Mr., Yarnscombe.
Chammings, Mr., Beaford.
Champion, Madame, Barnstaple.
Channel, Mrs., Richmond.
Chanter, J. H., Esq., Barnstaple.
Chanter, Rev. J. W., Ilfracombe.
Chapel, Mr., Torrington.
Chapel, Miss,   „
Chapman, Mr., Black Torrington.
Chapman, Mrs., Sheepwash.
Chappel, Mr., Black Torrington.
Chapple, Mr., Southmolton.
Charlewood, Admiral, Northam.
Chevalier, Mr., Liverpool.
Chevalier, Mr., Manchester.
Chichester, Capt., Bickington.
Chichester, C., Esq., Barnstaple.
Chowins, Mrs., Torrington.
Christopher, Mrs.,   „
Churchill, Miss, Barnstaple.
Churchward, Rev. Dimond, Northam.
Clare, Rev. R., Appledore.
Clarke, Mr., Bideford
Clarke, Mr., sen., Torrington.
Clarke, Mrs., Merton.
Clarke, Mrs., Wear Gifford.
Clements, Mrs., Yarnscombe.
Coates, Mr., High Bickington.
Cock, Mr., jun., Southmolton.
Cocks, Mr., Torquay.
Coffin, Pyne, J., Esq., Bideford (2).
Colby, Rev. E. R., Torquay.
Cole, Mrs., Southmolton.

Cole, Miss, St. Giles'.
Colemb, Col., London.
Coles, Mrs., High Bickington.
Colin, Mr., Torrington.
Collihole, Mr. T., Winkleigh.
Collihole, Mrs.,   „
Collin, Miss, Torrington.
Colwill, Mr., Torrington.
Colwill, Mr. T., Ilfracombe.
Colwill, Mrs. W., Torrington.
Comins, Mrs., Southmolton.
Cook, Mr., Appledore.
Cook, Mr., Barnstaple.
Cook, J., Esq., Barnstaple.
Cooke, J., Esq., London.
Cooke, Rev. Canon, Exeter.
Coombe, Mr., Exeter.
Coombe, Mrs., Torrington.
Cooper, G. Groves, Esq , Bideford (2).
Cooper, Miss, Monkleigh.
Copp, Mr., Beaford.
Copp, Mr., Torrington.
Copp, Mr. J.,   „
Copp, Mrs., Peter's Marland.
Copp, Mrs , Torrington.
Cork, Mrs., Monkleigh.
Cormer, G., Esq., Mold.
Cotton, —, Esq., Exeter.
Couch, Mr., High Bickington.
Cowell, Mr., Westward Ho !
Cowling, Mr., Barnstaple.
Cox, E., Esq., Bideford.
Cox, Mrs., Yarnscombe.
Crang, Mrs., Barnstaple.

LIST OF SUBSCRIBERS.

Crang, Mrs., Thorne.
Criddle, Mrs., Exeter.
Croft, W. C., Esq., Westward Ho !
Crooke, Mr., Instow.
Croscombe, Mr., Roborough.
Crossman, Mr., Bideford.
Cruwys, Mr., Bideford.
Cudmore, Mr., Merton.
Cull, Mr., Torrington.
Culliford, Rev. V. H., Winkleigh.
Currie, Miss, Ilfracombe.
Curtis, Mr., Barnstaple.
Curtis, Miss, Lankey.

Dalby, Mr., Torrington.
Dalby, Rev. F. H., Barnstaple.
Darracott, Mrs., Appledore.
Davey, G., Esq., Bradiford.
Davey, Mrs., Buckland Brewer.
Davidson, J. B., Esq., London.
Davies, Mr., Barnstaple.
Davies, Rev. D. B., Braunton.
Davies, Mrs., Swansea (2).
Davis, Mr., Torrington.
Dawe, Mr., Barnstaple.
Dawe, Mr., Exeter.
Dawson, J., Esq., London.
Day, Mrs. A., Appledore.
Day, Mr. G. H., Braunton.
Deane, A., Esq., Webbery, Bideford.
Dendle, Mr., Barnstaple.
Dennis, Mr., Hunshaw.
Dennis, Mr., Barnstaple.
Dennis, Mrs., ,,

Didham, Capt., Bideford.
Dilling, Mrs , Barnstaple.
Dillon, Mr , Taunton.
Dingwell, Mr., Barnstaple.
Docker, Mr., Torrington.
Dodd, Mr., Castle Hill.
Doe, G., Esq., Torrington.
Doe, Mrs , Chas.,   ,,
Doe, Miss,   ,,
Doidge, Rev. J., Southmolton.
Dodge, S , Esq., Torrington
Dowding, Rev. T.,   ,,
Dowell, Mrs., Bideford.
Down, Mr., Bickington.
Down, Mrs., High Bickington.
Down, Miss, Cardiff (10).
Down, Miss, Bideford.
Down, Miss, London.
Downing, Mr., Hatherleigh
Downing, Mr., Wear Gifford.
Downing, Mrs. J., ,,   ,,
Downing, Mr. R., Atherington.
Downing, Miss, Torrington.
Drake, Mrs., Braunton.
Drake, Miss,   ,,
Dredge, Rev. J. T., Buckland Brewer.
Drew, H., Esq., Exeter.
Drew, J., Esq.,   ,,
Dufty, T., Esq., Winkleigh.
Dunn, Miss, Northam.
Dunning, Miss, Winkleigh.
Dyer, Mr. R , Braunton.
Dyer, Miss, Southmolton.
Dymond, Mr , Bideford.

Earl, A., Esq., Black Torrington.
Eastmond, Mr., Bideford.
Edger, Miss, Pilton, Barnstaple.
Edwards, Rev. E., Torquay.
Edwards, J., Esq. Barnstaple.
Edwards, Mr., Petrockston.
Edwards, Miss, Torrington.
Eland, Mr , Exeter (2).
Eland, Rev. J., Bideford.
Elias, J. R., Esq., Pentraeth
Ellacombe, Rev. H., Clyst St. George.
Ellis, Rev. J., Appledore.
Ellis, Mrs., Westward Ho !
Embery, Mrs., Bideford.
Essery, Mr., Hatherleigh.
Evans, Mr , Dolton.
Eveny, F., Esq. Exeter.
Eyre, Mrs. F. T., Instow.

Fairchild, Mr., Great Torrington.
Fairchild, Mr., Torrington.
Farleigh, Mr.,   ,,
Farleigh, J., Mr., Barnstaple.
Farringdon, Mrs., London.
Featherstone, Mr., Bideford.
Fergusson, Miss, West Linton, Scotland.
Finch, Mr., Exeter.
Fisher, Mr., Barnstaple.
Fisher, Mr., Frithelstock.
Fisher, G., Esq., Torrington.
Fisher, T., Esq., Buckland House
Fisher, Mrs., Huntshaw.
Fisher, Mrs., Northam.
Fisher, Miss, Frithelstock.

Fisher, Miss, Pilton, Barnstaple.
Fitze, Mrs., Exeter (2).
Fleck, Mr., Bideford.
Folland, Mr., Barnstaple.
Folland, Mr., Dolton.
Folland, Mr., Torrington.
Follett, C., Esq., Exeter.
Folley, Mrs., Torrington.
Forest, Mr., Barnstaple.
Foster, R., Esq., Torrington.
Foweraker, Rev. E. T., Exeter.
Fowler, Rev. H., Gloucester.
Fowler, Rev. N., Utting (2).
Fowler, P., Esq., Mold.
Fowler, Mr., H.,   ,,
Fowler, Mrs., Torrington.
Fowler, Miss,   ,,
Fox, J. B., Esq., Ilfracombe.
Foxwell, Mrs., Torrington.
Frances, C., Esq., Ilfracombe.
Frances, Mrs., Westward Ho !
Fraser, Mrs., Instow.
Freeman, Mrs., Torrington.
Freeman, Miss, Frithelstock.
Friend, Mr., Dolton.
Friend, Mr., Braunton.
Friend, Mr., Winkleigh.
Friendship, Mrs., Torrington.
Friendship, Miss, Torrington.
Froude, Mrs., Barnstaple.
Fry, Mr., Wear Gifford.
Fry, Miss, Bickington.
Fulford, Mr., Bideford.
Fulford, Mr. E., Buckland Brewer.

LIST OF SUBSCRIBERS.

Fulford, E. J., Esq., Exeter.
Fulford, R W., Esq., Exeter.
Fulford, Mr. T., Buckland Brewer.
Furse, E., Esq , Southmolton.
Furse, Mrs., Torrington.
Furse, Miss, Pilton, Barnstaple.
Furseman, Mrs., Langtree.
Fursey, Mr., Appledore.
Fursey, Mr., Jun., Appledore.
Furze, Miss, Torrington.

Galliford, E., Esq., Southmolton.
Gamble, C., Esq., Barnstaple.
Gammon, Rev. J., Shebear.
Gard, Mr., Yeovil.
Gardener, Mrs , High Bickington.
Gardener, F , Esq., Ilfracombe.
Gatenbury, Miss, Braunton.
Gawtry, Miss., Torrington.
Gaydon, Mr., Kingston-on-Thames.
Gaydon, Mr., Barnstaple.
Gaydon, Mr. G. T., Barnstaple.
Gayton, Mrs., High Bickington.
Gaywood, Mr., London.
Geoeghan, Mr., Bideford.
Gilbert, Mr., Exeter.
Gilbert, Miss, Black Torrington.
Gill, Mr., High Bickington.
Gill, Mr., Torrington (2).
Gill, H. S., Esq., Tiverton.
Gimblett, Mr., Crediton.
Glubb, W., Esq., Torrington.
Glyde, Mr., Barnstaple.
Godfrey, Mr., Castle Hill.
Goman, Mr., Bideford.

Gomer, Mrs., Wear Gifford.
Good, Mr., Southmolton.
Goode, Mr , St. Giles'.
Goodwin, A., Esq , Ilfracombe.
Gordon, Capt , Appledore (2).
Gordon, Mr., Castle Hill.
Goss, Mrs., Merton.
Gossett, Rev. J., Westward Ho !
Gould, Mr., Barnstaple.
Gould, Mr. G. H., Barnstaple.
Gould, G., Esq., Hatherleigh.
Gould, R., Esq., Barnstaple.
Gould, W., Esq , Ilfracombe.
Gowman, Mrs., Appledore.
Grant, Mr., Torrington.
Granville, Rev. R , Bideford.
Greek, Miss, Barnstaple.
Green, Mr , Exeter.
Gregory, Mr , Bideford.
Gregory, Rev. R., Tavistock.
Gregory, W. H., Esq., London
Gregory, Mrs. M. A., Barnstaple.
Gribble, J , Esq , Barnstaple.
Grigg, Mr., Parkham.
Guard, Mr., Torrington.
Guest, Mrs., Bristol (2).
Guille, Mrs., Rectory, Great Torrington.
Gunn, Mr., Exeter.
Gunn, Mr., Torrington
Gurney, Rev. W., Roborough.

Hackwill, Mrs., Langtree.
Hagley, Mrs , Torrington.
Hall, Rev. W. C., Pilton, Barnstaple.

LIST OF SUBSCRIBERS.

Hames, Mr., Braunton.
Hamlyn, Mrs., ,,
Hamlyn, Mrs., Thorne.
Hancock, Mrs., Pilton, Barnstaple.
Handcock, Mr., Little Torrington.
Handford, Mr., Torrington.
Handford, Mr. H., Taunton.
Handford, Mr. T. E., Torrington.
Harding, Col., Pilton, Barnstaple.
Harding, Mr., Exeter.
Harding, Mrs., Barnstaple.
Harper, J., Esq., ,,
Harpley, Rev. J., Tiverton.
Harris, Mr., Bideford.
Harris, Mr., Exeter (2).
Harris, Rev. E., Exeter.
Harris, J., Esq., ,,
Harris, W., Esq., Braunton.
Harris, W. P., Esq., ,,
Harris, Mrs., Appledore.
Harris, Mrs., Buckland Brewer.
Harris, Mrs., Merton.
Harris, Mrs. S., Roborough.
Harris, Miss S., ,,
Harriss, Mr., Barnstaple
Hart, Mrs., Stevenstone.
Hartnoll, Mr., Braunton.
Hartnoll, Mr., Barnstaple.
Haslam, T. W., Esq., Westward Ho!
Hatherley, J., Esq., Bideford.
Haverfield, Mrs., Torrington.
Hawker, Rev. Treasurer, Ilfracombe.
Havel, Mrs., London (2).
Haydon, Mrs., Langtree.

Heale, Mrs E, Fremington.
Heale, Mr. G. A., Parkham.
Heape, Mr, Braunton.
Heard, Mr., Beaford.
Hearn, Mrs., ,,
Hearn, Mrs. S, Barnstaple.
Hearn, Miss, ,,
Heather, Mr., ,,
Heddon, Mrs., Braunton.
Hemans, Mrs., High Bickington.
Hencott, Mr, Exeter.
Henry, Rev. J., Southmolton.
Hensley, Rev. E, Parkham (2).
Herniman, Mr., Pilton, Barnstaple.
Heywood, Mr., Bideford.
Heywood, Mr., Torrington.
Heywood, Mrs., Plymouth.
Hick, Mr. C., Black Torrington.
Hiern, J., Esq., Barnstaple.
Higman, Rev. R, Torrington.
Hill, Mr., Barnstaple.
Hill, Mr, ,,
Hill, Mr, Southmolton.
Hockley, Major, Barnstaple.
Hodge, Miss, Braunton.
Hodge, Mrs., Torrington.
Hodges, Mr., Bideford.
Hogg, Mr, ,,
Holderness, Rev. W, Woolfardisworthy.
Hole, C., Esq., Bideford.
Hole, T, Esq., Ilfracombe.
Hole, Mrs, Beam House, Torrington.
Hole, Mrs, Torrington.
Hole, Miss, ,,

LIST OF SUBSCRIBERS.

Hole, Miss D., Torrington.
Holland, Miss, Bickington.
Holwill, Mr., Torrington.
Holwill, Miss, Bideford.
Honey, Mr., Hatherleigh.
Hookway, Mr., Bideford.
Hookway, Mrs., Kingscott.
Hooper, S., Esq , Hatherleigh.
Hooper, Mrs., Exeter.
Hooper, Mrs , Exeter.
Hore, Rev. W. S., Barnstaple.
Horn, Mrs., Black Torrington.
Horn, Mrs.,   ,,   ,,
Horner, Mrs., Barnstaple.
Hosken, Mr., Lankey.
Hoskins, Mr., Marazion.
How, A., Esq., Barnstaple.
How, J., Esq., Bideford.
How, Mr., Little Torrington.
Howard, Mr., Braunton.
Hughes, J. C., Esq., Caersws.
Hugo, W. J., Esq., Barnstaple.
Hurdon, Rev. J., Barnstaple (2).
Hussey, Mr., Wrafton.
Huswaite, Mr., Buckland Brewer.
Hutchings, J., Esq., Torrington.
Hutchings, Mr. Lee, Bideford.
Hutchinson, General, Northam.
Huxtable, Mr., Southmolton.
Huxtable, Mrs., Langtree.

Ireland, Mr., Barnstaple.
Irish, Mrs., Barnstaple.
Isaac, Mr., Roborough.

LIST OF SUBSCRIBERS.

Isaac, Mr., Winkleigh.
Isaac, Mrs., Hatherleigh.
Isaac, Mrs., Wear Gifford.

Jackson, H., Esq., Barnstaple.
Jackson, J., Esq , Croydon.
Jackson, Mr., Torrington.
Jackson, Mr. J., „
Jackson, Mr. T., „
Jackson, S , Esq , Pembroke.
Jackson, Mrs., London (2).
James, Mrs , Glenburnie, Bideford (2).
Jardine, Rev. —, Great Torrington.
Jarman, Miss, Northam.
Jenn, Mr., Black Torrington.
Jewell, Mr., Torrington.
Jewell, Mr. H , Parkham.
Joce, Mr., Bideford
Johns, Mrs., Torrington.
Johnson, E , Esq., Farringdon House, Exeter.
Johnson, Mrs , Cross, Little Torrington (2).
Johnson, Miss, Rosemoor, Torrington (2).
Jones, Rev. R , London.
Jones, Dr , Torrington.
Jones, Mr. „
Juniper, Mr., Stevenstone.

Kay, —, Esq , Barnstaple.
Kearsley, G., Esq , Exeter.
Kelland, Mrs., Southmolton.
Kellow, Mr., Bickington
Kelly, Mr., Black Torrington.
Kemp, Miss, Merton.
Kempe, Rev. Prebendary, Merton
Kempe, A., Esq , Exeter.

LIST OF SUBSCRIBERS.

Kempe, Mrs., Bideford.
Kennard, Mrs., Taunton (2).
King, J. R., Esq., Crediton.
King, Mr., Ilfracombe.
Kingdon, Mr., Torrington.
Kingdon, J. A., Esq., Southmolton.
Knight, Mr., Torquay.
Knill, Mr., Barnstaple.
Knill, Mr., Pilton, Barnstaple.
Knill, Mr. T. J., Barnstaple.
Knott, Mr., Stevenstone.

Laffere, Mr., Hatherleigh.
Lait, W., Esq., Torrington.
Lake, Mr. J., London.
Lake, Mr. J.,   ,,
Lake, Mrs., Buckland Brewer.
Lamperd, Miss, Torrington.
Lamping, Mr., Braunton.
Landon, Rev. C., Ashford.
Landon, Rev. J. W., Braunton.
Lang, Rev. Dashwood, Instow.
Langbridge, Mr., London.
Langdon, Rev. A., High Bickington.
Langdon, Mrs., Braunton.
Latey, John, Esq., London.
Law, Dr., Barnstaple.
Lawrence, Mr., Torrington.
Leathern, Mrs., Northam.
Lee, Mr., Torrington.
Lemon, Mrs., Appledore.
Lemons, Mrs., Atherington.
Lendon, Mr., Exeter.
Lethaby, R. P., Esq., Barnstaple

Lethbridge, Mr., Exeter.
Lethern, Miss, Winkleigh.
Ley, Mr., Barnstaple.
Ley, Mr, Langtree.
Ley, Mr. T., „
Lile, Mrs., Barnstaple.
Lind, Mrs, Bideford.
Lind, Mrs., Northam (2)
Linington, Mr, Winkleigh.
Lipscombe, J., Esq., Exeter.
Literary Institution, Barnstaple.
Littlejohns, Mrs., Exeter.
Littledale, Rev. C., E. Kingscott.
Littleworth, Mr., Barnstaple
Lock, G., Esq , Instow.
Lock, T., Esq., „
Loftus, Mrs., Croydon.
Loveband, Rev. W A., Pilton.
Loveband, Mrs., Torrington.
Lovelace, Mrs., Plymouth.
Lovell, Mrs., Frennington.
Lovering, Mrs., Braunton.
Lownes, Rev. J., Bideford.
Lownes, Rev. W., „
Lucas, Mr., Torrington.
Ludlow, Rev. A., Northam.
Lukey, Mr. W., Plymouth.
Luxton, Mr., Winkleigh.
Luxton, G , Esq., Winkleigh.
Luxton, Mrs., Hatherleigh.
Luxton, Mrs. T., Winkleigh.
Lyddon, Mr., jun., Southmolton.
Lyne, Mr., Dolton.
Lyne, Mrs., Petrockstow.

LIST OF SUBSCRIBERS.

Macartnay, Major, Torrington.
MacDonald, Rev. A., Barnstaple.
MacGregor, Mrs., Bideford.
Mackay, Mrs, Barnstaple.
Mackay, Mrs., London.
Mackelvie, Torrington.
Mackencie, Mr., Barnstaple.
Maine, Mrs., Atherington.
Maine, Mrs., Northam.
Maine, Miss, Bideford.
Majendie, Rev. C. W., Barnstaple (2).
Mallett, Mr., Torrington.
Mallett, Mrs., Frithelstock.
Mallett, Mrs., Swansea.
Mallett, Mrs., Torrington.
Manley, J., Esq , London.
Manning, Mr., Barnstaple.
Marks, G., Esq , Beaford.
Marsh, Mr., Barnstaple.
Marsh, Mrs. S. W , Barnstaple.
Marshall, Rev. J., Beaford.
Marshall, T., Esq., Barnstaple.
Martin, Mr., Barnstaple.
Martin, Mr., Parkham.
Martin, Mrs., Wear Gifford.
Mason, Mrs., Langtree.
Mathews, Mrs. S , Appledore.
Mathews, Miss, Petrockstow.
May, Mrs., Exeter
May, Mrs., London (2).
May, Mrs., Stevenstones.
May, Mrs., St. Giles'.
May, Mrs., Torrington.
Medland, Mr., Torrington.
Muxworthy, Mr., Barnstaple.

Miller, J., Esq , Barnstaple.
Miller, Mr., Winkleigh.
Millett, Colonel, Wear Gifford (4).
Mills, A., Esq., Bude.
Mills, Mr., Langtree.
Mills, Mrs., Marland.
Mills, Miss, Torrington.
Milroy, J , Esq., Barnstaple.
Milton, Miss, Barnstaple.
Milton, Miss, Southmolton.
Mitchell, C., Esq., Dolton.
Mitchell, Mr. S., Winkleigh.
Mitchell, Mrs , Barnstaple.
Molesworth, General, Kenwith, Bideford.
Molesworth, Mrs., Kenwith, Bideford.
Molland, Mr., Winkleigh.
Monkleigh, Mr., Bideford.
Moon, Mrs., London.
Moor, Mr , Southmolton.
Moore, Mr., Barnstaple.
Moore, Mrs.,   ,,
Moore, Mrs , Torrington.
Morgan, Rev. J., Dolton.
Morley, Mr., Torrington.
Morris, Mr., Langtree.
Mortimer, —, Esq., Barnstaple.
Mortimer, Mr., Petrockstow.
Morton, F., Esq., Southmolton.
Mosley, Mr , Hatherleigh.
Mountjoy, Mr., Bradiford.
Mountjoy, Mr. G., Southmolton.
Mules, Mr., Southmolton.
Murphy, Mr., Bideford.
Murray, Mr., London.
Muxworthy, Mr., Yarnscombe.

Nance-Rievel, Mr., Langtree.
Nance-Rievell, Mrs., Kingscott.
Narraway, Bideford.
Nations, Mr., Torrington.
Neale, Rev. E. S., Exeter.
Nicholls, Mr., Bristol.
Nicholls, Mr, Winkleigh.
Nichols, Mr., jun., Bristol.
Nichols, Mrs., Langtree.
Nightingale, Rev. T., Exeter.
Noble, Rev. R., Torrington.
Norman, J. H., Esq., Winkleigh.
Norman, Mrs., Monkleigh.
Norman, Mrs., Westward, Ho!
Norman, Miss, London.
Northcote, Mr., Petrockstow.

Oatway, Mr., Bideford.
Oatway, Mr.,   ,,
Oatway, Mr. R., Yarnscombe.
Oatway, Mrs., Yarnscombe.
Oldham, E. J., Esq., Hatherleigh.
Oliver, W., Esq., Barnstaple.
Oliver, Mrs., Bideford.
Owen, A. W., Esq , Black Torrington.

Page, Mrs. J., Roborough.
Palmer, Colonel, Torrington.
Palmer, Rev. C.,   ,,
Palmer, C. E., Esq., Barnstaple.
Pardon, Mr. H., Winkleigh.
Pardon, Mrs. R., Roborough.
Parfitt, Mr., Exeter.
Parks, Mr., Barnstaple.

Parminter, Mrs., Pilton, Barnstaple.
Parr, Mr., Sheepwash.
Partridge, Mrs., Monkleigh.
Passmore, Mr., Buckland Brewer.
Passmore, Mr., Exeter.
Passmore, Mr., Southmolton.
Passmore, Mrs., Torrington.
Passmore, Mrs. J., Peters Marland.
Pearce, Mr., Barnstaple.
Pearce, Mr., High Bickington.
Pearce, Rev. J., Hatherleigh.
Pearce, Mr., Yarnscombe.
Pearce, Mrs., Pilton, Barnstaple.
Pearce, Mrs., Torrington.
Pearse, J., Esq., Hatherleigh.
Pearse, Mrs., Northam.
Pearse, Mr., Exeter.
Peake, Mr., Barnstaple.
Peake, Mr., High Bickington.
Peake, Mrs. Plymouth.
Peake, Mrs., Southmolton.
Pease, Miss, Darlington (2).
Pedlar, C., Esq., Bideford.
Pedlar, Mrs. R., High Bickington.
Peel, C., Esq., Saint Giles'.
Pengelly, Mr., Yarnscombe.
Pengelly, W., Esq., Torquay.
Penhale, Mrs., Barnstaple.
Penleaze, Rev. J., Black Torrington.
Pennington, Mr. A., Parkham.
Pennington, Mrs., Northam.
Perking, Mr., Wear Gifford.
Perry, Mr., Torrington.
Petherick, J. W., Esq., Exeter.

Petter, Mr., Barnstaple.
Petter, Mr., jun., Ilfracombe.
Pettle, Mr., Torrington.
Pettle, Miss, Ashford.
Phare, Mrs., Hatherleigh.
Phillips, Mrs., Torrington.
Phillips, Miss, London.
Pidgeon, Mr., Torrington.
Pigott, Rev. T. F., Fremington.
Pike, Mrs., Bideford.
Pinkett, Mrs., Barnstaple.
Pinkett, Mrs., Instow.
Pittwood, Mrs., Hunshaw.
Plimsoll, Dr., Exmouth.
Pollard, Mr., jun., Bideford.
Ponsford, Mrs., Pilton, Barnstaple.
Pope, T., Esq., Exeter.
Pope, Mrs., Merton.
Pope, Mrs., Torrington.
Popham, Mrs., Appledore.
Pound, Mr., Bideford.
Powell, B., Esq., Mold.
Power, J., Esq., Northam.
Prance, Mrs., Appledore.
Pratt, Dr., Appledore.
Pratt, Dr. C.,   „
Pratt, Mrs., Darlington.
Pratt, Mrs., Winkleigh.
Predeaux, Mr., Barnstaple.
Price, Dr., Ilfracombe.
Price, C., Esq., Westward Ho ! (2).
Price, W. E., Esq., Torrington (2).
Pronger, C. E., Esq., Barnstaple.
Prouse, Mr., Bideford.

Puddicombe, Mrs., Bideford.
Puddicombe, Miss, Pilton, Barnstaple.
Pulsford, Mr., Barnstaple.
Pynsent, G., Esq., Westward Ho !

Quance, Mrs., Merton.
Quick, Miss, Instow.
Quicke, Mrs , Exeter.

Rafferelle, Mr., Barnstaple (2).
Ramson, J. L., Esq., Sidmouth (2).
Ratcliffe, Mrs., Barnstaple.
Rawle, Mrs S.,   ,,
Raymond, Mr., London (2).
Reed, Mr., Torrington.
Reed, Rev. W. B., Holsworthy.
Rendell, J. M., Esq , Exeter.
Restarick, Mr , Bideford.
Rew, Mr., London.
Reynolds, Rev. C., Appledore.
Riccard, R. M., Esq., Southmolton.
Richards, Mr., Devonport.
Richards, Mr., Exeter.
Richards, Mr., High Bickington.
Rickard, Mrs., Bideford.
Ridge, Mr., Petrockstow.
Ridley, Mr., Bideford (2).
Righton, Mr., Northam.
Roberts, Mr., Exeter.
Roberts, Rev. E., Braunton.
Robertson, Mr., Little Torrington.
Robins, W., Esq., Ilfracombe.
Robins, Mrs., Buckland Brewer.
Robinson, Capt., Braunton.

LIST OF SUBSCRIBERS.

Rock, W. F., Esq., Blackheath (16).
Rockhey, Mr., Barnstaple.
Rockhey, Mrs., Roborough.
Rodd, Mrs., Northam.
Rogers, T., Esq., Orleigh Court, Buckland Brewer.
Rooker, J., Esq., Bideford.
Rose, Miss, Exeter (2)
Rough, Mrs., Winkleigh.
Rounsefell, Rev. B., Plymouth.
Rouse, L., Esq., Sheepwash.
Rouse, Mrs., Torrington.
Rouse, Miss de St. Vincent, Barnstaple.
Rousham, P., Esq., Torrington.
Row, Mr., Kingscott.
Rowe, Mr., Barnstaple.
Rowe, W., Esq., Barnstaple.
Rucker, Miss, London.
Rucker, Miss A., London.
Rudall, Miss, Sheepwash.
Rudd, Mrs., Torrington (2).
Ruddle, T., Esq., Shebear.
Rude, Mr., Barnstaple.
Rude, Mrs., Torrington.
Rush, Mr., Barnstaple.
Russell, Colonel, Barnstaple.
Russell, Rev. J., Swymbridge.
Russell, R. R., Esq., Atherington.
Russell, Mr. W., Atherington.
Rutter, Miss, Cork (4).
Rutty, Rev. J., Barnstaple.

Sage, Mr., Bristol.
Sandercock, J., Esq., Northam.
Sanders, Miss, Hatherleigh.

Sanders, Mrs., Instow.
Sanders, Mr., Southmolton.
Sandford, Mr., Torrington.
Sandford, Mr. R., „
Sandford, Mrs , „
Sandford, Miss, „
Sangster, Captain, Northam.
Salter, Mr , Torrington.
Sargent, Mrs., Leamington.
Satterley, Mr., Barnstaple
Saunders, Mr., jun., Northam.
Saunders, Mr C., Buckland Brewer.
Saunders, Mr. J., „ „
Saunders, Mrs., Langtree.
Sawer, T., Esq., Northam.
Saxon, Mrs , Barnstaple.
Scott, Captain (Smytham), Little Torrington.
Scott, Mr., Hatherleigh.
Scott, Mr., Kingscott.
Scott, Rev. T., Bideford.
Searle, Mr., Barnstaple.
Seldon, Mr., „
Seldon, Mr., Lankey.
Seldon, Mr. T. P., Barnstaple.
Sellick, Mr., Bideford.
Sellick, Mr., Plymouth.
Sellick, W., Esq., Taunton.
Sergent, Mrs , Alwington.
Sewell, Mrs., Barnstaple.
Seymour, Rev. E. A., Barnstaple.
Shackerley, Mrs., Ilfracombe (2).
Shapland, Dr. D., Croydon.
Shapland, Mr., Wear Gifford.
Shapland, Mr. A., Barnstaple.

LIST OF SUBSCRIBERS.

Shapland, H., Esq., Pilton, Barnstaple (4).
Sharpe, Mr., Stevenstone.
Shaw, Rev. J., Torrington (4).
Shearm, Mr., Beaford.
Shedlock, Mr., Bideford.
Shepherd, Mrs., High Bickington (2).
Short, Mr., Wear Gifford.
Short, Mrs., Merton.
Short, Mrs., Torrington.
Short, Mrs.,   ,,
Shute, Mr., Buckland Brewer.
Sidgwick, Rev. J. B., Hunshaw.
Sillifant, Mr., Frithelstock.
Sillifant, Rev. C. W., Wear Gifford.
Sillifant, J., Esq., Wear Gifford.
Sillifant, T., Esq., Eggesford.
Sing, Mr., Torrington.
Sinkins, Mrs., Bideford.
Skemp, Rev. C., Newcastle-on-Tyne (2).
Skinard, Miss, Instow.
Slade, D., Esq., Ilfracombe.
Sleath, J., Esq., Barnstaple.
Slee, Mr., Torrington.
Slee, Mrs. J., High Bickington.
Slocomb, Mrs., Thorne.
Sloggett, Mr., Bristol
Slowman, Mrs., Barnstaple.
Smale, C., Esq., Bideford.
Smale, Mrs., Hatherleigh.
Smith, Heywood, Esq., London (2).
Smith, Mr., Torrington.
Smoldon, Miss, Castle Hill.
Smyth, Mr., Barnstaple.
Snell, Mrs., Little Torrington.

LIST OF SUBSCRIBERS.

Snow, T., Esq., Exeter.
Snow, Mr., Southmolton.
Soady, Mrs., Brooking, Ilfracombe.
Somes, Mrs, Annery, Bideford.
Southcott, Miss, Southmolton.
Spear, Rev. J., Modbury.
Squire, Mr., Langtree.
Squire, Mr., London.
Squire, Mr., Wear Gifford.
Squire, Mr. C., Bideford.
Squire, Mr. J, Bideford.
Squire, Miss, Torrington.
Stabb, T., Esq, Ilfracombe.
Stafford, Mrs., Dolton.
Stapleton, Mr, Merton.
Stevens, Mr., Barnstaple.
Stevens, Mr., Litton.
Stevens, Mr, Taddiport
Stevens, Mrs. Moore, Winscott, Peter's Marland.
Stewart, Mr., Barnstaple.
Stewart, Mr. J., Barnstaple.
Stiff, Mrs., Barnstaple.
Stockham, Mrs., Exeter.
Stone, Mr., Bideford.
Stoneham, P., Esq, Ilfracombe (2).
Stoneman, Mr., Torrington
Stoneman, E., Esq., Plymouth.
Stoneman, Mr., Merton.
Strang, Mr., Hatherleigh.
Studdy, J., Esq., Buckland Brewer.
Sully, Mr., Exeter.
Sutcliff, Dr., Torrington.
Symons, Mr, Barnstaple.
Symons, Mr., London (2).

Swinburn, Mr., Southmolton.
Symons, Mrs., Fremington.

Tanner, Mr., Southmolton.
Tanton, Miss, Bideford.
Tapley, R. L., Esq., Milton Damerel.
Tapscott, Mr., Exeter.
Tatham, Mr., Barnstaple.
Taylor, H. Lowman, Esq., London (2).
Telfer, Rev. E. A., London (4).
Thelwell, Rev. T., Westleigh.
Thiers, Mrs., Appledore.
Thomas, Mr., Ilfracombe.
Thomas, H. D., Esq., Exeter.
Thomas, J. L., Esq., ,,
Thomas, Mr., Pilton, Barnstaple.
Thomas, Rev. W. G., St. Asaph.
Thompson, Dr., Bideford.
Thompson, Rev. D., Atherton.
Thompson, J., Esq., West Buckland.
Thorne, J. A., Esq., Barnstaple.
Thorne, Mr. R., Langtree.
Thorne, Rev. S. L., Bradford.
Thorne, Mr. W., Langtree.
Thorne, Mrs., Bickington.
Tilke, Mrs., Peter's Marland.
Till, Mrs., St. Giles'.
Todd, G., Esq., Bideford.
Toller, W. H., Esq., Barnstaple.
Toms, Mr., Torrington.
Townsend, Mr., Exeter.
Trace, Mr., Petrockstow.
Tremear, Miss, Torrington.
Trickey, Mr., Merton.

LIST OF SUBSCRIBERS.

Tucker, Mr., Bideford.
Tucker, Mr., Exeter (2).
Tucker, Mr., Petrockstow.
Tucker, Mr., Peter's Marland.
Tucker, Mr. J E., Langtree.
Tucker, Pitts, Esq., Barnstaple.
Tucker, Mr. W., Appledore.
Tucker, Mrs, Buckland Brewer.
Turner, Mr, Winkleigh.
Turner, G., Esq., Bideford.
Turner, Mrs., Dolton.
Turrall, Mr, Torrington.
Turton, Mrs., Ilfracombe.

Underhill, Mr., Exeter.
Upstyle, Mrs, Torrington (2).

Vanstone, Mr., Black Torrington.
Vanstone, Mrs., Instow.
Vaughan, Mr., Torrington.
Veale, Mrs., Hatherleigh.
Vellacott, Mr., Bideford.
Venner, Mr., Southmolton.
Verney, Miss, Wrafton.
Vibert, Miss, Bideford.
Vicary, Mr, Merton.
Vicary, T., Esq., Plymouth.
Vidal, E., Esq., Cornborough, Bideford.
Vincent, Mr., Bideford.
Vinson, Mr,   „
Vodden, Miss, Kingscott.
Vodden, Miss, Torrington.
Vye, Captain, Ilfracombe.

Wadham, Mrs., Darlington.
Wagner, J. H., Esq., Barnstaple.
Walche, Mrs. Devenish, London.
Wallop, The Hon. John, Eggsford.
Walters, Mr., Langtree.
Ward, Mr., Merton.
Ward, Mr , Petrockstow.
Ward, Mr., Torrington.
Ware, C., Esq., Exeter.
Warman, Mrs., Wear Gifford.
Watson, Rev. J., Torrington.
Watts, Mr., Barnstaple.
Watts, Miss, Torrington.
Way, Mrs., Braunton.
Way, Mrs., London.
Weatherall, Mr., Bideford.
Webber, Mrs., Atherington.
Welch, T., Esq., Ilfracombe (2).
Wells, Mrs.,   „
West, T., Esq.,   „
Westacott, Mr., Barnstaple.
Westacott, Mrs., Torrington.
Westacott, Miss, London.
Westaway, Mr., Merton.
Westaway, Mr., Torrington.
Westcott, Mr., Beaford.
Westlake, Mrs , Torrington.
Weston, C., Esq., Exeter (2).
Whale, Rev. J., Dolton.
Wheatley, Miss, Stevenstone.
Wheaton, Mr., Exeter.
Wheeler, E. G., Esq., Little Silver.
Whitchurch, Mrs., Barnstaple.
White, Mr., Torrington.

LIST OF SUBSCRIBERS

White, R., Esq., Instow.
Whitlock, Mr , Parkham.
Whitlock, Mrs., Langtree.
Whitmore, Mr., Torrington.
Widicott, Mr., Buckland Brewer.
Widlake, Mr., Roborough.
Willett, Rev. C., Saltreen, Monkleigh
Willett, Mrs.,   „   „
Williams, Mr. H. R., Barnstaple.
Williams, Miss, Herts
Williams, Miss, Winkleigh.
Willis, Mr., Petrockstow.
Wills, C., Esq , Dursley.
Wills, I., Esq., Plymouth.
Wills, T., Esq., Brighton.
Wills, Mrs., Barnstaple.
Wills, Miss, Torrington.
Willshire, C., Esq , Barnstaple.
Wilson, Mr , Bideford.
Wilson, Mr., Castle Hill.
Wilson, Mrs., Little Torrington.
Wilson, Miss, Torrington.
Winter, Mrs.,   „
Withecombe, Mrs., Buckland Brewer.
Wolstenholme, Miss, Alverdiscott.
Wonacott, Miss, Atherington.
Wonnacott, Rev. J., Exeter.
Wood, Mr , Bideford.
Wood, Miss N.,   „
Wood, Rev. W. J., Atherington.
Woodgate, Miss, High Bickington.
Woolcombe, Rev. Archdeacon, Exeter.
Wooley, Rev. W. S., Bideford.
Woolner, Rev. J., Exeter.

LIST OF SUBSCRIBERS.

Worth, Mr., Exeter.
Wreford, Mr., ,,
Wren, Major, Northam.
Wren, Mrs., ,,
Wright, Mrs., Black Torrington.
Wylde, Miss, London.

Yeateman, Rev. R., Frithelstock.
Yeo, Mr., Bideford.
Yeo, Miss, ,,
Yeo, Mr. C., Torrington.
Youatt, Mr., Monkleigh.
Youings, Mr., Barnstaple.
Young, Mr., Bideford (2).

BIBLIOLIFE

Old Books Deserve a New Life
www.bibliolife.com

Did you know that you can get most of our titles in our trademark **EasyScript**™ print format? **EasyScript**™ provides readers with a larger than average typeface, for a reading experience that's easier on the eyes.

Did you know that we have an ever-growing collection of books in many languages?

Order online:
www.bibliolife.com/store

Or to exclusively browse our **EasyScript**™ collection:
www.bibliogrande.com

At BiblioLife, we aim to make knowledge more accessible by making thousands of titles available to you – quickly and affordably.

Contact us:
BiblioLife
PO Box 21206
Charleston, SC 29413